FABRICE HADJADJ

THE RESURRECTION

Experience Life in the Risen Christ

Scriptural passages are taken from *The Jerusalem Bible* translation, often with the author's revisions.

Publisher: Pierre-Marie Dumont
Editor: Romain Lizé
Copyediting: Janet Chevrier
Iconography: Isabelle Mascaras
Layout and cover: Elena Germain
Production: Pascale van de Walle, Thierry Dubus

Original French title:
Résurrection : mode d'emploi
© 2016 by MAGNIFICAT SAS, 15-27, rue Moussorgski, 75018 Paris

Copyright © 2016 by MAGNIFICAT Inc. All rights reserved.
Printed by Imprimerie Marquis, Canada
Edition number: MGN16006
ISBN: 978-1-941709-22-1

www.magnificat.com

FABRICE HADJADJ

THE RESURRECTION

Experience Life in the Risen Christ

Translated by
Michael J. Miller

MAGNIFICAT

Paris • New York • Oxford • Madrid

The gift of opening our eyes

Archbishop Charles J. Chaput, O.F.M. Cap.

You have in your hands a brilliant little book. Saying that though is dangerous. "Brilliance" in a text, like the beauty of opera and ballet, may be admirable. But for ordinary humans like you and me, it can also be annoying. Worn out at the end of a day, and amply reminded of our shortcomings by the problems of work and family, the last thing most of us need is an invitation to mental gymnastics.

Fabrice Hadjadj understands. One of Europe's leading philosophers, Hadjadj is a writer, speaker, and public intellectual of exceptional skill. But he's also the father of four daughters and two sons, and the husband of a gifted actress—thus entangling him every day in peace negotiations among children, overdue bills, family schedules, and apologies to his wife for mistakes he can't remember making. In a word, he is *Catholic*, a man with a mind and soul hungry for the transcendent; and a heart and hands covered in the raw material of daily life. He connects with "ordinary" believers because he is one.

Just as God took on human flesh in his Son Jesus Christ, so the work of Hadjadj is profoundly incarnational. He honors God's thunder on Sinai and the radiance of Christ's Transfiguration. But his real interest lies elsewhere. He notes that "there is something better than doing extraordinary things: illuminating ordinary things from within." He turns the reader again and again toward reading Scripture in a new light. Hadjadj wants us to see the power of God in his humility, simplicity, and restraint; to find the miraculous in the small and the ordinary; to encounter God in the routines and the beauty we take for granted. Moses parts the Red Sea with his staff. This is a great miracle. But the greater miracle takes place when the God who created the oceans asks a Samaritan woman for a drink of water.

Hadjadj focuses here on the Resurrection. His grasp of Scripture leads to some extraordinary reflections on the meaning of time, money, food, the body, motherhood, death, technology, sexuality, even papal leadership. His chapter on "myrrh-bearing women" is rich with a wonderful Christian earthiness and wry humor, firmly rooted in reality. "Romantic passion," he writes, "requires much less love for the other and death to oneself than daily fidelity. . . . Tristan and Isolde could kill themselves together. But much more strength is needed to live together, to hand on life together, and even to be raised up together and to have to put up with each other for all eternity." I know quite a few (happily) married couples who would agree.

In an age of unbelief, Hadjadj notes:

[T]he event of Someone rising from the dead seems difficult to swallow for someone who is used to avatars, online profiles, and

3-D objects that are neither born nor dead nor alive. But for a positive fellow of yore who was good with his hands, a peasant, a miller, a tanner, [resurrection] was unlikely no doubt, and yet no sooner did he hear, "Truly, truly, I say to you, unless a grain of wheat falls into the earth and dies, it remains alone, but if it dies, it bears much fruit" (Jn 12:24), than it became a simple matter; it was as true as April, the renewal of the greenery, the gold of the harvest . . . .

For Hadjadj:

In the age of the Apostles, [people's estrangement from the natural] world was rarer; then they had the valley of the Jordan, not Silicon Valley. Today, the spade, the fishnet, the shepherd's crook or the [carpenter's] plane seem more than ever to be a prerequisite of the apostolate. The meaning of the Incarnation involves the meaning of the flesh, since openness to the supernatural does not distort nature but rather returns us back to its source. Anyone who has not experienced the order of things with his own hands can only pay lip service in preaching the One who orders these things. He is not realistic enough to bear witness to the Resurrection.

And so on. Hadjadj has a rare talent for tying multiple sources of scholarship and experience together to make biblical passages come intensely alive. In practice, he's the shrewdest, most subversive sort of catechist. Hadjadj smuggles a caravan of deep, faithful, provocative thinking into the reader's head, disguised by vivid examples and easy writing. Encountering his work is a bit like getting rain after a long, hard drought. The heart, like dry soil, soaks up the words.

It's one of God's little ironies that France—self-consciously secular France—should produce one of the finest Catholic minds in decades; a mind equally at ease with the Word of God, the grandeur of fine art, dilemmas in philosophy, and the awkward, miraculous travails of marriage and family life.

But as Hadjadj himself reminds us, we worship a God intimately aware of our joys and sorrows. We worship a God who knows the smell and feel of our world not from the outside, but from walking its hills; a God full of surprises and overflowing with love for his creation. What Fabrice Hadjadj accomplishes in these pages is very simple and enormously difficult at the same time: He helps us open our eyes to the presence of God right in front of us. Would that we all had that gift.

✠ Charles J. Chaput, O.F.M. Cap.
Archbishop of Philadelphia

TABLE OF CONTENTS

Introduction.. 17

Principle of reality 18

Reality at its source.. 21

Glory and routine.. 23

Getting up in the morning 25

A bit like a user's guide 28

I. Your money or your life 31

An imitation of the three theological virtues............ 33

Trader or witness?.. 36

Buyer or heir?... 39

The virtual and the living 41

The future and what is to come, balance sheet and

memorial... 43

II. The myrrh-bearing women 47

Anointing the Anointed One..................................... 49

Love like myrrh 52

The courtesan, the mother, the wife.......................... 54

Fear of the resurrection.. 56

III. The head-cloth in its place.................................. 59

"After you" 61

A miracle in the hollow 63

Like a mother.. 65

Housekeeping 67

IV. Go down and see if I'm there 71

Non-recognition... 73

Transmitting the untranslatable................................. 75

Return from Eden 77

The problem of the Incarnation 79

To open our eyes 81

The largest in the smallest 83

V. Do you have something to eat? 85

Beauty secret 87

Dependence and assumption 89

The law of the table 92

He who eats my flesh and drinks my blood 94

VI. In accordance with the Scriptures 97

A vain message and an illegible presence 99

The descendant's Ascension 101

The One who sums up and redeems history 103

Letting the Bible read us 106

VII. Out of breath: saying good day and forgive me 109

Against devotional dualism 113

The cure: saying "Good day" and meaning it 114

So supernatural and so routine 116

The more truth there is, the more need of forgiveness 117

VIII. Place your hand in my side 121

I am like Saint Thomas 122

A hothead 124

Eternal wounds 126

If we denied a single fact about this world 128

He who doubted in good faith 129

IX. Back to fishing 133

And the Word was made carpenter 136

Media man and medieval man 138

Father vinedresser 140

Fishers of sinners 142

X. Papal indignity 145

Triple trouble 147

The joy of feeling unworthy................................... 150

The happiness of accusing oneself........................... 152

Being a (Holy) Father.. 154

XI. To all creation 157

If it is a creature... 160

In him all things hold together 162

Turns and detours of Providence 164

All the world and the kingdom of those near and dear........ 167

XII. Laying one's head on the chopping block (or handing over one's body to be stoned) 171

Stephen, Saul, and Ananias..................................... 174

Proposing a toast 176

Power of prayer 178

More radical than a jihadist 180

Epilogue... 183

So that we might be human..................................... 184

Faced with counter-annunciations........................... 186

The apparitions of the Risen One as our temptation in the desert 188

To the reader of self-hell(p) books,
This little book about heaven-help.

Ah! how dazzling it would be if, at that very moment, as we were being nailed up, there should escape, gush from the coffin, the miraculous trill of a flute!... What a surprise!... Ah, what a lesson for families!... The first Mr. Kick-the-Bucket not having lived in vain, having finally surprised, understood, all the graces of springtime!... Revolutionary of the Shades! Troubadour in the Sepulchers! Buffoon yodeling in the Caverns of the World!... I'd like to be that fellow! What an ambition! My only one, by Gosh!

Louis-Ferdinand Céline, *Guignol's Band*, vol. I

I have always been a believer. Which is quite understandable: I come from a rather atheistic family. Therefore I believed at first in my parents, as though they were gods (I did not have to topple that idol; it fell quickly enough by itself). I also believed in Raffi when he crooned, "Baby Beluga." I believed in the Incredible Hulk, a.k.a. Bruce Banner, whose swelling green muscles would rip his clothes when he got angry. I believed in Charles Ingalls and his *Little House on the Prairie* (but for too short a time—alas, I was living in the midst of the high-rises of La Défense, a modern business district in Paris). I believed that food grew right there in the supermarket display cases (and I still have a lot of trouble imagining the time actually required for a turkey to be fattened or an apple to ripen). I believed in the French Revolution and in the Socialist Revolution, although my father was

17

a member of a moderate labor union, at least by French standards. . . .

Soon I believed in Nietzsche, certain that I was *Beyond Good and Evil*, and in the libertine author Georges Bataille, although a bit too timid to commit myself entirely to the discipline of orgies. Then I believed in Hegel, so as to try to recapitulate all the previous moments of my belief, then, upon returning from "absolute knowledge," I believed in the novelist Céline, preaching the gospel of the *Journey to the End of the Night*. At the same time I believed in Zen Buddhism—I admit it—and I sat on the floor with business managers and menopausal school-teachers to accept the marvel of my inner emptiness. In all those phases, of course, I believed a lot in myself, and, above all, I believed that I was not a believer.

And one fine day, whoosh! All this mysticism was swept away by the torrent of life. I rediscovered the fact that I was Jewish and French, only to discover soon afterward, in old books written in French, that God had become a Jew. So then I became a Christian. And even Catholic. That was the end of the time when I was so credulous. And the beginning of a very profound—and humiliating—objectivity.

Principle of reality

My faith in a certain Galilean carpenter named Jesus, who died and rose from the dead in Jerusalem *under Pontius*

Pilate—in other words, in a little province of the Empire governed by a minor official of the Roman administration—was very effective at putting my feet back on the ground. This faith is too detailed to let us hover among the abstractions of the "sciences" or the "spiritualities." The fact of the Resurrection, above all, is a rather severe principle of reality. Those who believed in it were fishermen who knew how to repair their nets, stonemasons capable of building cathedrals, monks skilled in clearing and tilling fields—which is to say: very practical, down-to-earth people. Believing in the Risen Lord was for them as solid as planting wheat or constructing a Romanesque basilica. Even more solid, since they relied on that faith to raise vaults as well as grain.

The Easter Gospels are all along these lines. They rub our illusions the wrong way. Unfailingly, if we had to imagine for ourselves a man who had entered into divine glory, we would think of him accomplishing extraordinary things—gleaming brighter than a celebrity at the Oscars, juggling stars, establishing such harmony that *the wolf dwells with the lamb, and the leopard lies down with the kid* (cf. Is 11:6). . . . Now, you have to admit, the risen Jesus does nothing of the sort. Except for a net filled to bursting point with fish and an Ascension on which two men dressed in white threw cold water by asking the eyewitnesses, *Why do you stand looking into heaven?* (Acts 1:11), he performed hardly any miracles. Or, if he did perform any, they were sort of miracles in reverse, tending to be more discreet, reserved, ordinary.

Curiously, after his Resurrection, not only was he less resplendent than at his Transfiguration on Mount Tabor, he did not even have his former charisma any more: Mary Magdalene mistook him at first for a simple gardener; the disciples on the road to Emmaus, for the most ignorant of the inhabitants of Jerusalem; the Apostles, for some sort of retired fisherman on the shores of the Sea of Galilee. . . . He crossed over into death, he arose again from hell, and, in spite of it all, with inexplicable restraint, he insists on manifesting himself as a passerby. The Evangelists emphasize this modesty: *Jesus stood among them* (Lk 24:36; Jn 20:19 and 26). *Among them* means with a surprising familiarity, more surprising than any fantastic apparition, because, in that state of affairs, a fantastic apparition is what one might have expected.

And people expect this fantastic apparition to the point where they no longer read what is written: they suppose that he walked through walls, that he uttered esoteric words, that he presented himself as an escape artist with superpowers in a halo of light. But no. He was simply there. He said to them, *Peace be with you*, which is the equivalent of saying "Good evening." He broke bread, ate some grilled fish, shared their meal. He commented on Scripture for them the way we tell at table about an adventure that has recently happened to us. And instead of making a show of strength for them—for example by bending an iron bar through the power of thought—he showed them his wounds. In ordinary miracles, the wounds disappear; here, they remain, eternally.

Reality at its source

After all, there is something better than doing extraordinary things: illuminating ordinary things from within. And Jesus cannot do otherwise if he is indeed the creative and redemptive Word—the same one who creates, the same one who saves, and the same one who saves what he has created, without which he would save nothing (no *tabula rasa* [blank slate] here, but a table that takes up the *fruit of the earth and work of human hands*). He was the one who invented ordinary things, like something no one had ever done before—so how could he despise them? He ransoms them, therefore, lifts them up and reveals the fantasy in them. Of course, now and then he indulged in impressive miracles, quite a few of them, in fact, such as healing the sick by the mere contact of his garment, or feeding thousands of hungry people with what might have served as a snack for two. But we must admit, on the scale of his stay here on earth (a few moments out of the three years of his public life as opposed to thirty years of hidden and silent life), and especially for someone who is almighty, these are, all in all, rather limited effects. And with good reason! If he had made an entire city spring up from the ground, people would run the risk of forgetting that he has already created the whole universe. If he had raised roofs with a snap of his fingers, we would wind up no longer understanding that he had created far better than that right from the start: human beings, with all their body parts, who, with the energy that he gives them, practice the art of carpentry. Moses can open up the Red Sea with his staff. Jesus, as the eternal Word, is the author of the Red Sea itself, down to the tiniest gleam of its smallest wave, so that the most surprising thing about him is not parting it with a gesture or calming the storm (what could be more natural?), but asking the Samaritan woman for a drink of water.

Then too, his miracles always end up downplaying the spectacular. The Redeemer could not eclipse the Creator, since they are one and the same God. This is why the purpose of his extraordinary acts is not to turn people away from what is ordinary, but, in his unfathomable origin and providence, to bring them back to it. When he restores sight to the blind man, it is so that he might marvel at seeing like everyone else. When he cures Peter's mother-in-law, it is so that Peter might admire his mother-in-law (a miracle of a different order!). When he summons Lazarus from the tomb, it is so that Lazarus can then die again—for good.

Office hours are necessary to allow for the unexpected encounter. But there's nothing stopping us occasionally deviating from the timetable to give meaning to a punctuality that might eventually seem mechanical and fastidious to us. A kindly school principal who has set up a daily schedule can, by way of exception, suspend it so as to host a little impromptu celebration where he will recall that, if the bell rings, it's not to have the students get back in line, but to allow for just such an improbable confrontation between a bewhiskered teacher and a dunce in a baseball cap, who would otherwise never have dreamt of such an encounter. . . . Thus a miracle suspends the ordinary course of things only to open our eyes blinded by routine and to unveil the gift hidden behind the usual grind. It springs more directly from the source of reality than reality itself: reality then lifts its skirts to reveal a glimpse of its dizzying originality. There is nothing more normal than to see what's right under our noses: it no longer astonishes us. But when by a miracle the man born blind starts to see just like everyone else, sight appears to us as just what it really is: a gift that comes from the invisible One. And thus, by the same reasoning, the mother-in-law appears as a blessing from the Eternal One, and death as the possibility of the supreme offering. . . .

Glory and routine

We are touching here on one of the most important problems of existence, something resembling the squaring of the circle, which we could call the reconciliation of glory and routine. No doubt there is a certain mediocrity in being content with what is routine, and to have no ambition whatsoever for glory. But there is also something base about rejoicing in glory and basking in the spotlight while being no longer capable of gratitude for the sunlight each day. How many artists have found inspiration because they wanted to spare themselves the bother of vacuuming? How many philosophers forged mighty theories about Man because they wanted to avoid the inconvenience of living with a woman? Conquerors have built empires out of an inability to cultivate a garden. Writers have produced masterpieces out of fear of raising children. As for future supermen, they are of course the most inept of all. Their bionic prostheses know nothing of the revolution of a simple caress or the happiness of fashioning a piece of furniture by hand. If they seek permanent Internet connections and memories of 1,000 petabytes, it is because they have never known how to *look at the birds of the air* or to *consider the lilies of the field* (Mt 6:26-29). And they hope to become immortal, thanks to round-the-clock medical supervision, because they have nothing for which to give up their life. (This is why these immortals will not live as long as many mere mortals: rather quickly they will wish to consign themselves to the latest, most progressive form of euthanasia.) Their obsession with superpowers is the mark of their powerlessness: they never manage to conceive of the incredibility of the visible world, the present of each presence, the impressiveness of each impression, the sensational in each sensation. . . .

The Risen Lord is not one of those supermen. His glory espouses the everyday. Scarcely has he attained the pinnacle of perfection than he finds nothing better to do than to meet with his friends for conversation and a meal. He insists on showing that he is simply human, and that alone would be enough to prove that he is God (for a simple human being would, above all things, not want to appear simply human; he even would have the annoying tendency to make a fuss so as to appear *like a god*). The Risen One does not juggle stars, because the stars are already the works of his hands. He does not gleam like a film star because he wants to light up the sorry mug of the first comer. And he already makes *the wolf dwell with the lamb, and the leopard lie down with the kid,* since he sends his disciples *as lambs in the midst of wolves* (Lk 10:3) and he makes me lie down faithfully with my wife.

Getting up in the morning

This then is the thesis that structures this little book: the apparitions of the Risen Lord have an eminently practical character. They are not phantasmagorical escapes from the here and now in order to speculate on what is far off; they lead us back to love of neighbor, teach us to see things *from above*, that is, to see the same things as the common of mortals, but to see them from the Spirit. John observes that therein lies the essential: *As yet the Spirit had not been given, because Jesus was not yet glorified* (Jn 7:39). And Jesus specifies this in his Last Discourse before his Passion: *It is to your advantage that I go away, for if I do not go away, the Counselor [Paraclete] will not come to you; but if I go, I will send him to you* (Jn 16:7).

Easter reaches its fulfillment in Pentecost. One can go forth from Egypt, but this liberation would be a total disaster if each Hebrew left slavery behind only to become a little Pharaoh. One can marvel at the victory of the Risen One, but this Ascension would be a great fall if the believer got rid of his fear of death only to become a monster of pride, to despise the works of the Creator, and ignore the humility of the Messiah. The glorification of Jesus must lead to the disappearance of the Risen One and to the sending of his Spirit, who enlivens everyday routine by the fact that he is poured forth from and toward the Ineffable.

The verbs that we solemnly translate as "rise (again)" (*egeirō, anistēmi*) refer in Greek to ordinary actions: getting up, awakening, standing up. The angel Gabriel speaks them to Joseph: *Rise, take the child and his mother* (Mt 2:13). Jesus uses them in speaking to the paralytic: *Rise, take up your pallet and walk* (Mk 2:9). What could be more commonplace than standing on your own two feet? Only an ex-paralytic can remind us that this is a privilege. Doubly a privilege if you add his arms, and the fact that he has gone from being bedridden to being a stretcher-bearer (what the experienced stretcher-bearer often forgets, thinking himself in the position of a helper, is that he is above all someone helped by God). For the stretcher that recently carried him, the former paralytic now carries as an emblem of this incomparable delight. In this he is stronger than the cyborg who is bored with having legs and wants jet engines instead.

Similarly, what is more ordinary than being a father? Even our own father managed it, which is saying a lot! And so we easily believe it much better to be an expert in a particular field, preferably an innovative one. And yet neither Joseph nor Mary worked in this sort of line. Their holy family reminds us that, more than any technological or even artistic invention, fatherhood and motherhood are eternal fulfillment and newness. Angels descend from heaven for such commonplace things, whereas they do not budge for the fabrication of a superior artificial intelligence (unless perhaps to bug it).

When a machine is perfected, it is above all so that we can remain under the blankets and amuse ourselves with escapist films. But the fact that Christ rises is first and foremost so that we might get up in the morning, quite simply, in thanksgiving—something no fancy Nespresso coffee-maker suffices to do.

A bit like a user's guide

There is already a publication entitled *Suicide: A User's Guide*: it catalogues rather quick techniques for stopping your heart or blowing your brains out. Alas, with the resurrection we cannot claim such efficiency. Although it is relatively easy to put an end to one's own life, it is on the other hand much harder to get it to start again. You do not pull yourself up from six feet under the way you throw yourself out of a sixth-story window. I am capable of removing myself from the company of the living; not of raising myself from the dead.

This impossibility corresponds, however, to another very widespread impossibility: that of giving life to oneself. Indeed, it is just as impossible to raise oneself from the dead as to give birth to oneself. And yet—an incredible thing for our pride!—we are born. Someone will no doubt reply that giving birth to oneself is impossible for man as an individual, but not for man considered as a species (since we have already given birth, obviously, to a number of children), whereas to raise from the dead is impossible for the species as well as for the individual. To that I will reply that the analogy certainly has its limits, but that, in a certain no less essential respect, it leads us instead to assert that it is more impossible to be born than to be raised from the dead, and, moreover, this is why the most advanced technology tends to fabricate individuals rather than let them be born—and, it must be said, it can be excused for that.

Consenting to being born is more fundamental and more difficult, basically, than consenting to resurrection. First, being born of Jane and Robert is less exalting than being reborn directly from God. Secondly, to welcome the joy of life in heaven supposes already having welcomed some kind of *joie de vivre*, even though we are still here on earth, and live caught between the motorway and the supermarket. Why would we desire for eternity a life that we dislike? What good is the miracle of resuscitating if there is not the wonder of being born? And at the same time, it is faith in this miracle that pushes us to recognize this wonder. To accept our birth into this place and this time with this far from dreamlike body and this sad environment only to end up very probably dying like a dog, it is necessary no doubt to believe that there is some kind of providence behind it all. It is the resurrection, ultimately, that makes birth seem to us not in vain (religions that reject the resurrection generally see birth as a scourge or a fall; and their followers do not commit suicide above all because the only thing that could truly satisfy them would be not to have been born at all). The fact remains that in faith in the resurrection, as in consent to one's birth, the same openness to life is in play—to life as something that anticipates us and always surprises us.

This book will therefore not "make it work" (for that, you would be better off with the directions for a computer or a gun). Its only aim is that we might be truly alive, so that an event might be more important than its result, and an encounter more than a recipe.

I

YOUR MONEY OR YOUR LIFE!

Some of the guard went into the city and told the chief priests all that had taken place. And when they had assembled with the elders and taken counsel, they gave a sum of money to the soldiers and said, "Tell people, 'His disciples came by night and stole him away while we were asleep.' And if this comes to the governor's ears, we will satisfy him and keep you out of trouble." So they took the money and did as they were directed; and this story has been spread among the Jews to this day.

Matthew 28:11-15

People always mention Judas' thirty pieces of silver, never the soldiers' *sum of money* (more precisely, the Greek text reads "a sufficient number of silver pieces"). Now which of these two pecuniary arrangements is more serious—the one that handed Christ over to the cross or the one that obliterates his glory? Isn't the second more extreme than the first? Doesn't money show a greater power to fascinate when it offers to betray a resurrected man, and not just a mortal? It is fitting, in any case, to linger over this final episode involving finances, which is also Saint Matthew's last word on the subject. Earlier, when Jesus had sent the Apostles on a mission, he had commanded them: *Take no gold, nor silver, nor copper in your belts* (Mt 10:9). Even before that, on the Mount, he had declared: *You cannot serve God and mammon* (Mt 6:24).

We could not have thought of it on our own: isn't money an instrument, and isn't it a question of making "good use" of it? It is at our service, and we should not serve it. It can't buy happiness, no doubt, but "it contributes to it." Why does Christ liken it to a sort of spiteful person? Why does he impute intentions to it, to the point that he describes it as "unjust," or, in some translations, *deceitful* (Lk 16:11)? If it is only a tool of commerce, how could it change into the boss? I'm willing to admit that we have less of a grip on a banknote than on a hammer: it is a paper instrument that tends to slip through our fingers. It is nevertheless a tool, one that is more effective than a hammer at almsgiving, buying fine lingerie, or even shutting someone's trap. . . . After all, wouldn't Christ have been more prudent had he made his emissaries employees and given them a little pocket money for their petty travel expenses, to make them a little more independent too (like our politicians)? Don't tell me that the man who could multiply loaves so easily could not multiply coins! How is it that he does not do what alchemy has always dreamed of: to transmute mud into gold? How is it that he, who has no fear of touching lepers, has this absurd fear of being contaminated by money?

Fortunately, some churchmen have made progress in this area. Isn't it necessary to have the *means* to preach that God is *great*? And yet, in the passage we are discussing, the acceptance of the *sum of money* corresponds quite precisely to the rejection of the Resurrection.

An imitation of the three theological virtues

The encyclopedias tell us: money (which is not always silver) has three functions. It is a "measure of value," a "store of value," and a "medium of exchange."

As a "measure of value" it is a unit of account that enables us to balance completely different things and thus to avoid the perplexity that would come over us at the moment of a transaction if we were to ask a question such as: How many hours of babysitting is this pair of shoes worth? The question is all the more delicate because the saleslady may not have any children. Thanks to money, the motley actions and objects of this world are converted into precise quantities (so many seashells yesterday, so many dollars today), and these quantities make it possible to equalize values. Nothing is incomparable any more, therefore, and we have here a "measure for everything," a "universal equivalent" that not only spares us the difficult questions mentioned above, but also gives us the pleasant assurance of saying, after a quick calculation, "One square foot in New York City is worth 975 Italian sausages," or even: "A general practice doctor is worth three cashiers."

As a "store of value," money allows us to defer the acquisition of goods over time. For it is not wealth in itself, but a means of obtaining it. Money is always something else: it is not what it is—a disk of metal or a slip of paper—that we find so arresting about it, but rather what it is not, what it enables us to have. In this sense, it has no odor of its own (it does not give off the aroma of a food), yet it can make us salivate over all sorts of merchandise that can be purchased with it. Because of this power to buy something as a future possession, it obtains something for us right away: the ability to dream about everything that one might shortly choose to treat oneself to: this handsome coat, this family vacation, this tantric massage, the latest Smartphone (but wait a while, a more sophisticated model will come out soon). Avarice is the fixation of this waking dream, purse in hand. The avaricious person rejoices in all the purchases that he could make, and in order to keep them all within reach of his pocket, he makes none of them.

This does not prevent us from acknowledging that money is above all a medium of exchange. It facilitates exchange because of its aforementioned functions, but also because it is manageable and divisible. If I wanted to have a livelihood for a year by giving up the use of my house for that amount of time, it would be necessary for the butcher, the baker, the street vendor, the sous-chef at the fast-food restaurant, the Apple store clerk, etc., to be able to come and live there, taking turns or simultaneously, which would give them the opportunity for close encounters they really don't want at all. . . . Therefore, it is better for me to move into an apartment and to convert this house into money, which I will exchange for their goods and services. This shows that this "medium of exchange" is more than a medium: it tends to exchange the usage value for the exchange value itself, reducing your house to a piece of merchandise, transforming all the most valuable things that you might do and have into the ability to acquire what has a more or less expensive price tag. This is true because, although the absence of money reduces you to being only able to do things yourself, the abundance of it obliges you *not* to do things any more and *not* really to use things any more, but rather to buy ready-made products and endlessly replace them.

That being the case, it is curious that the three functions that we have just mentioned correspond, as though by chance, to the three theological virtues—faith, hope, and charity (and this correspondence is no doubt what enables money—a talent, a mite, or a drachma, according to the parable—to serve as a metaphor for grace). Whereas faith allows us to consider every being as a fantastic creature beloved by the eternal Father, money as a measure of value makes us regard them as an article with a price. Whereas hope opens us up to unexpected beatitudes, money as a store of value guarantees us access to the offers at a shopping mall. Whereas charity results in the communion of persons, money as a medium of exchange presides over the circulation of merchandise.

Trader or witness?

Now we can guess why the pieces of silver accepted by the guards *are sufficient* to hide the truth *to this day*. What they experienced near the tomb was *a great earthquake* which *rolled back the stone* barring the entrance to the tomb, and the vision of someone whose *appearance was like lightning. . . . And for fear of him the guards trembled and became like dead men* (Mt 28:2-4). There is nothing very comfortable about an experience like that—especially at dawn after a boring night keeping watch, when you are getting ready, not for a cataclysm that wakes the dead, but for the changing of the guard so that you can go home and get some sleep. And so, in order to avoid a lot of trouble, so as not to have to testify to something that is beyond them and would put their social situation at risk, they gladly admit that all that glitters is not glory and spread a good old *story* about burglary while they slept.

The term translated here as "story" is *logos*, or, actually, *ho logos*: the word. In contrast to the incarnate Word, therefore, here we have the monetized word. It is not so much a matter of *not believing* in the Resurrection as of *making people believe*—and this is of capital importance, so to speak—in the removal of corpses. You just can't escape the necessity of believing (as we saw in the introduction). But either you believe in the logos without money (*Every one who thirsts, come to the waters, even if you have no money. . . . For thus says the* LORD: *'You were sold for nothing, and you shall be redeemed without money'*, Is 55:1; 52:3); or else you believe yourself and seek to make others believe with the logos of money (*Those who lavish gold from the purse, and weigh out silver in the scales, hire a goldsmith, and he makes it into a god; then they fall down and worship!* Is 46:6). This logos of money has the advantage of being quantifiable and, above all, quantifying. It puts you in control rather than into a relationship of trust. With it, you do not found your existence on faith in a life that is stronger than death, but on belief in theft, in necessary exploitation, in the inevitable trafficking in bodies, while we sleep peacefully in our beds.

This is the credulity that is lavished, I won't say by money in itself, but by the *love of money*, as Saint Paul says (1 Tm 6:10). It allows you to be a *trader* and protects you from being a *witness*. The trader works in impersonal domination, in the bottom line, in calculated anticipation. He speculates about figures and cannot waste time considering the workers who are behind them. One click, and there's a good transaction made! It makes little difference what really happens to the carcasses— the people who are fired, the families that are hungry, the cultures that are devastated—it even makes little difference whether they are dead or alive, provided that they bring in a profit. There are *values*, of course; but in fact, that's all there are: they entirely cover up the *living*. Now, you can survey their trends, by the values, you can foresee their development, do business with them, derive a profit from them, but how do you expect to follow on a computer graphic the unique adventure of every poor fellow, of every plot of land, or of every hearth and home?

Where the witness is content to receive something given, the trader, for his part, builds a fortune. He increases his buying power, and if his power to redeem ("without money") diminishes as a result, then come what may! In the meantime, he is freer to acquire plenty of "revolutionary novelties." They numb him. Why should he worry that they deprive him of springtime, of the dawn, of this flower at the edge of the road, of this face at his side, and especially of his empty hands that could offer themselves, or finally of the joy of having few possessions, which brings out the resource of being and receiving that which is priceless? Why should he notice that his magical freedom works only on the market and therefore makes him subservient to it (*Whose likeness and inscription is this on the coin? Is it not Caesar's?* Mt 22:20-21)?

Buyer or heir?

And so King Ahab is rolling in dough and, on a sudden whim, he decides to buy with gold the vineyard of poor Naboth, because it is located not far from his palace and might make a pleasant vegetable garden for him. Now, even though he makes a considerable bid, and even offers to provide him with a "wine-growing parcel" that is ten times larger, Naboth inexplicably refuses: *The LORD forbid that I should give you the inheritance of my fathers!* (1 Kgs 21:3).

His vineyard is very small, but it is his. And not only in the sense of an interchangeable piece of merchandise, but as something that belongs to his history. His bunches of grapes are loaded with memories, of childhood games among the vine stocks, of his first labors alongside his father, of his sweat and blood, mingled with the sap depending on the seasons, the prunings and the grape harvests with his wife—who is perhaps dead now—or with his sons and daughters—who have since grown up, some of whom have already left home. . . .

For him, this vineyard is not only a possession, it is a presence. It is a thing and more than a thing—something a bit like his mother and like his child. He refuses to give it up, not because he is selfish or unadventurous, but because he is generous and welcoming. What would that vineyard be for Ahab? A pleasant view, a good without the goodness of an offering, a decorative addition without memories, a property without appropriation. It would belong to him on the land register but not in his heart. It would be part of his "having"; it would not be part of his being. Furthermore: having no roots in his being, this having would not really be his, and the king would naturally be inclined to sell it again for something else, another vineyard, another empty space. . . .

Money never makes something truly yours. It pays, but since it thus keeps you from paying personally, it precludes all deep ownership. In order for something to belong to us intimately, it has to escape us three times, it has to have been received as an inheritance from our fathers, it has to have been left as a legacy to our children, and, in the meanwhile, we have to have received it each day, surrounded by the cares of a humble, constant fidelity. This cannot be bought. This is received, then cultivated, and

finally left to others. This is like life—no, this is life.
It is really ours only when it has been received as a son
then given as a father, because we have believed in it and
we have cultivated it.

The virtual and the living

Basically, money and the resurrection are opposed as two
systems of possibility: the system of the virtual and the
system of the living. I am using the word "virtual" in a
very specific sense that does not encompass all sorts of
virtuality or fiction: there is a good virtuality and even an
excellent kind of dreaming that turns us away from reality
only to lead us back more deeply into it. The idea that we
would relate immediately and perfectly to existence from
the start is the fantasy of people who are sickened by their
excessive consumption of artificial things. For an animal
such as man, what is natural is affirmed by culture. We
need myths in order to enter into the logic of the living.
We need fairy tales in order to become realists. And, in order to reach the soul of reality, we need what at first glance
may seem to be a fairy tale but is really the Fact that surpasses all accounting—what may seem to be a myth but
is the adventure of the Logos himself: the News about the
Nazarene who died and rose again in Judea during the
governorship of Pontius Pilate.

What I am calling "virtual" here refers instead to
"virtual reality," in other words, to the opposite of myth,

41

poetry, and novels: a virtuality that tends to substitute itself for reality and to exert its influence over it. Digital
technology is in fact the ultimate stage of cash. The digita-
lization of the world through the Internet is the final step
in the monetization of the world through money. Here
dollars find their ultimate universal equivalent, the unit
for computing and appropriating all things. Reality, what
is given [*donum*], is systematically changed into *data*—in
exploitable databases (whereas myth, poetry, and novels
holistically give us a glimpse of the *donum*—the irreduc-
ible gift). Bodies lose their resistance and vanish into thin
air thanks to microchips; they are converted into bits and
pixels and placed at the disposal of our magic trackpad.
This virtual world provides us with permanent access to
other places and good deals. But it has lost what the living
world and beautiful stories offer us: proximity and event,
and even the event of proximity. For the virtual world of
Internet surfing, like an *Odyssey* with no return to Ithaca,
causes us to admire the movie hero and not to wonder at
our neighbor in the next seat, whereas all the events in
the Bible teach us that the person sitting beside us is more
important than the hero in the film—because they all
converge on love of neighbor. In order to reach our neighbor in his wondrousness, as we have already suggested, a
detour is necessary; one must take the longest route—by
way of a divine distance. Without this distance, what is
nearby is reabsorbed into the insignificance of the banal.

Now this distance of respect and wonder (the living system of possibility) is prepared, ultimately, by the mystery of the Risen Lord.

The virtual system, with its stolen bodies, does not allow us to receive life in its unlikely sudden appearances. For that, faith in this resurrection is necessary. Whereas money procures for us possibilities that we can grasp, the resurrection reveals to us a possibility that seizes us. Because the resurrection is for us impossible and inconceivable, it is true—with a truth that surpasses our powers and becomes their foundation in their openness to events. It teaches us that reality is first of all what we do not expect, that the past is much more than elapsed time, and that what is to come is more surprising than any future imagined by our science fiction.

The future and what is to come, balance sheet and memorial

These two systems of possibility are also two systems of time. In the first, time is regarded in terms of remunerative plans. We are in the *future*, in *what is going* to happen through our initiative. And this projection into the future implies a relation to the past as *balance sheet*: we keep accounts, we check results, we judge our own performance. The prevalent factor here is an intention to do business, which makes a person powerless to welcome an event or to evaluate it only as risk, accident, or waste.

In the second system, that of the resurrection, time appears messianic, it is ripped apart by the unexpected. We are in *what is to come*: not only *what is going* to happen through our initiative, but *what comes to us* despite ourselves. And this openness to what is to come implies a relation to the past as *memorial*: we remember that the most beautiful things that have happened to us, even if they are the product of our labor, have above all the character of a gift, of an encounter, of something undeserved. (The genius, as opposed to a merely talented person, always recognizes this: he regards his masterpieces as having issued from someplace higher than himself; this is always recognized by a lover too, as opposed to a mere partner: he always feels unworthy of the wife who lives by his side). The prevalent factor here is a desire for an openness that gives the strength to accept an event and to discern in it a sign, a grace, an addition.

Moses prays in a psalm: *So teach us to number our days that we may get a heart of wisdom* (Ps 90:12). This is because there is a wrong way to measure days, which corresponds to a wisdom with no heart in it: the measure of the future and of the balance sheet that can even contaminate Christians when they view eternal life as the result of moral planning. And then there is the true measure of days, which espouses the rhythm of the heart: this is the measure of what is to come and of what is past, which can touch even wrongdoers whose past then appears to them as marked by unexpected events, starting with that first, radical, absolutely undeserved event: their own birth.

The first system *buys* time: "Time is money." The second system *redeems* it: Redeem the present moment, *because the days are evil* (Eph 5:16). In following the second system, we recognize in the planting of the seed the tremendous promise of the tree; in the shrouding of the caterpillar, the promise of the butterfly; in the unexpected arrival of our in-laws, the promise of a celebration comparable to the Dionysia festival of antiquity where three tragedies were played, followed by a comedy. In the first system, one sees the same things, but in this estimation there is no esteem, only cognition without recognition and gratitude: one calculates the income that the seed will yield, one weighs the butterfly by its greater or lesser utility, one remains convinced that the arrival of the in-laws is a disturbance, unless there is some chance of doing business with one's father-in-law, or that Uncle Fred, who fortunately had no offspring, might remember us in his last will and testament.

Although planning is partly responsible for our survival, nevertheless, recognition of the unexpected is what makes us truly alive. And being truly alive is the ability to be suddenly hit by a car, but also the ability to become the friend of one's brother, the close companion of one's neighbor, or even to fall in love with one's wife (which is quite similar to the resurrection). One then discovers *the given* above and beyond the construct: grace above and beyond business, the priceless above and beyond the purchasable. But here's the thing: to avoid being hit by a car, one must also give up falling in love (which is almost the same thing anyway). They take the money from the high priests. They trade the Easter Gospel for the savings account booklet, faith in the resurrection for credit to spend on consumer goods. Even one's own birth is no longer acknowledged as a happy event. It is viewed instead as an unfortunate chance occurrence to be coped with as well as possible, by compensating oneself with distractions or by piling up fortunes. Besides, the wheeler-dealer imagines he was not born: he claims to have made his fortune by himself.

II
THE MYRRH-
BEARING WOMEN

When the sabbath was past, Mary Magadalene, and Mary the mother of James, and Salome, bought spices, so that they might go and anoint him. And very early on the first day of the week they went to the tomb when the sun had risen. And they were saying to one another, "Who will roll away the stone for us from the door of the tomb?" And looking up, they saw that the stone was rolled back; for it was very large. And entering the tomb, they saw a young man sitting on the right side, dressed in a white robe; and they were amazed. And he said to them, "Do not be amazed; you seek Jesus of Nazareth, who was crucified. He has risen, he is not here; see the place where they laid him. But go, tell his disciples and Peter that he is going before you to Galilee; there you will see him, as he told you." And they went out and fled from the tomb; for trembling and astonishment had come upon them; and they said nothing to any one, for they were afraid. . . .

Mark 16:1-8

One afternoon, when I was a student at the Institute of Political Science in Paris and had a cast-iron belief in nothingness, I climbed up on a table in the main hall and declared in an semi-loud voice to my fellow students: "Do you actually realize it? You will all die!" The exuberant vitality of my youth afforded me the great luxury of speaking about death as casually as a life-insurance representative. I took a wicked pleasure in mentioning its effects in detail—rotting flesh, worms eating your eyes, the earthly career that ends by leaving no trace in people's memories. . . . And so I tried to make more of an impression, to produce a little effect of my own. But the same youthfulness that allowed me to speak so readily about death just as easily allowed my listeners to ignore me.

The greenish ooze, the swarming vermin—they seemed not to worry about anything more than that; and, if they had had the patience to put their mental state into words, they might have replied: *What would this babbler say? He seems to be a preacher of foreign divinities. . . . We will hear you again about this* (Acts 17:18, 32).

In preaching nothingness, I thought that I was being profoundly anti-religious and, more particularly, anti-Christian. Yet there I was in a situation comparable to Paul's in the Areopagus. But these were different times: not only did they reject talk about the resurrection, they also rejected talk about death. In losing God, they had ended up losing atheism. In losing their wonder at the fact that we exist, they had ended up losing their anguish in the face of nothingness. It is not worth raising your head from your tablet—a tablet often livened up with series full of murders, the better to put the real corpses behind a screen.

So we dodge death, but the three myrrh-bearing women gently remind us: in order to ask yourself the question about the Risen One (to the point of being afraid of it), you have to be ready, not to "look Death in the face" (an abstract perspective by means of which philosophers excuse themselves from not looking their cousin in the face or even at their own face in a mirror), but rather to care about one dead person—someone heavy, palpable, beloved.

Anointing the Anointed One

The Shabbat had taken everyone by surprise. Jesus had been placed hurriedly in someone else's tomb, and they had not had the time to carry out the funeral rite for him. That had to wait until Saturday was over. This is already something remarkable, this sudden halt, this fidelity to the prescribed rest on the seventh day, even though they were responsible for this dead man at the end of the sixth. Wasn't there some urgency? Didn't they have to hurry *up*. No doubt, but someone who does not know how to stop does not "hurry up": he hurries *through*. He just keeps going forward—even when up against a wall, even on the brink of a chasm or—what is worse—over the back of someone weaker. He does not see that before making *something*, it is necessary to make *room*, it is necessary to stop being busy so that action can be orderly, with its proper direction, from its beginning to its end.

And so the women made room, but, as soon as the Shabbat was over, as one might expect, they quickly headed for the stores. Not to get a new dress or new sandals; rather—another classic purchase—to buy perfume. Recent scientific studies by renowned historians enable us to declare with certainty that these were not bottles of Dior, Chanel, or Guerlain. For, while Guerlain, Chanel, and Dior make excellent products for active women going to a board meeting or an evening out dancing, none, it seems, makes them for deceased sons. Now that is what these women were looking for—what today could be a whole new brand of cosmetics: perfumes for the young man who has been dead for three days.

That young man, whom they had followed from Galilee, had been struck down in mid-flight, condemned as a blasphemer, crucified between two thieves, and laid *in haste*—just as the Paschal lamb must be eaten, in haste (Ex 12:11)—in a tomb not carved for him—and now they were going to unseal that tomb, reopen the shroud and anoint the Anointed One (that is the meaning of the word "Messiah" or "Christ"). This contact with his body would make them unclean for a week. This uncleanness, however, would be quite the opposite of impiety. They were going to pay him their final respects, see his features from which the face had disappeared, apply their palms to his unfeeling skin, hesitate near the marks of the nails, feel the weight of his inert members, experience the horror of that mouth from which they had heard flowing the streams of Paradise, but which was now nothing but a nameless thing, less than a wound, a gaping grin soon to rot on the skull. They thought about all this as they went to the tomb, and also about their final gesture, which would be to wrap him up again like a baby in his swaddling clothes, and cast a final glance at this God who was now nothing more than a process of decomposition hidden in a package of white and perfumed cloths. . . . But none of that took place. As the first ones of all, they heard the incredible announcement that took away their mourning and left them with their jars of ointment still in their arms.

And this is why we have so much difficulty understanding this announcement: we lack the prerequisite condition for receiving it. I read somewhere that there was a little tribe in which a girl could not marry and have children unless she had first prepared the body of a deceased parent. A wise provision that one might reintroduce today to advantage. It is obvious enough that having felt the weight of a corpse makes you more inclined to live with a husband. Or even just to live with one's brothers. Ignatius of Loyola required his novices to wash the dead before pronouncing their vows (the Church, moreover, had elevated this final task to the rank of a "work of mercy"). In order to hear the announcement of the Resurrection, it is not enough to do yoga or to listen to conferences about spirituality: you have to be ready to enter into the tomb so eagerly that you give no thought to the stone closing it off, ready to touch the reality of death to the point of anointing decomposing flesh, ready to feel the weight of the absurdity of an innocent son crucified like a criminal. But modern comfort has deprived us of that preparation. We no longer take care of the dead members of our families by ourselves. We leave them to the funeral directors, who have made it their livelihood and handle the dead without love in exchange for money. We buy the services of funeral parlors. How then could we still be close enough to physical death to find ourselves in a place where a resurrection can surprise us?

Love like myrrh

Three Magi had come to Jesus' cradle. Three women come to his tomb. The Magi brought gold, frankincense, and myrrh. The women bring only myrrh (we can assume that their spices were made up of this resin from the balsam tree, which is preferably used, as its name indicates, for embalming). Now myrrh is the perfume of the Song of Songs. The bride sings: *My beloved is to me a bag of myrrh, that lies between my breasts* (Song 1:13). And the bridegroom replies: *I come to my garden* [recall that the Holy Sepulchre is located in a garden], *my sister, my bride, I gather my myrrh with my spice* (Song 5:1). This liquid perfume—the one with which the dead are anointed—is also the perfume of the life between the bride and the bridegroom.

And so the Bible is not to be recommended to Puritans: *My beloved put his hand to the latch, and my heart was thrilled within me. I arose to open to my beloved, and my hands dripped with myrrh, my fingers with liquid myrrh, upon the handles of the bolt* (Song 5:4-5). A league of decency would have to ban these verses. Indeed, they would be censored by a club of libertines as well. The myrrh is not a deodorant for petty seducers. It demands a *love [as] strong as death* (Song 8:6). This should not be interpreted too romantically. Rather, this is about ordinary married life. Romantic passion does not require as much love for the other nor death to oneself as does daily fidelity. Of course, Tristan and Isolde kill themselves together. But much more strength is needed to live together, to hand on life together, and even to be raised up together and to have to put up with each other for all eternity.

It is not insignificant, therefore, that the Risen One reveals himself in the first place to these three myrrh-bearing women who were faithful to him from Galilee to the defeat on Golgotha. *Male and female he created them* (Gn 1:27).

Male and female he recreates them. The light of glory does not abolish sexual difference. The Man *par excellence* turns first to a trinity of women. Indeed, if we are to believe the tradition associated with the Gospel according to Saint Luke, the revelation of the Risen One is made first to a couple—but separately (communion is strengthened only by rejecting the illusion of fusion): two angels announce it to women, one of whom is a certain Joanna (Lk 24:10), then Jesus manifests himself personally to the disciples on the road to Emmaus, one of whom is a certain Cleopas (Lk 24:18), who according to tradition is said to be Joanna's husband. Two separate encounters offering endless food for thought and conversation and, even more, the silence of the spousal bedroom.

The courtesan, the mother, the wife

The three women in our Gospel passage correspond to three major aspects of woman. The first Mary is distinguished by a place of residence, the second by a family tie, and the third by another name which is the very name of Salvation (Salome comes from *Shalom*, Peace, the first word of the Risen One to the Apostles). The woman designated by a place where you can always find her is the courtesan in her enclosed house. The woman designated by a tie that denotes her accomplishment is the mother— and the name of her son, Jacob or James, suggests a maternity that extends to all of Israel. The woman designated by a name that is a promise of what is to come for man is woman as such.

In married life, in motherhood, and even in prostitution, although in a deviant way, the feminine is manifested essentially, not as the ability *to do something*, but as the capacity *to receive someone*, to welcome another into herself, into her womb, whether it be for the seed, the fruit, or the stain. In her body, the woman welcomes the man; the mother welcomes the child; the prostitute welcomes the customers. This may explain a bit more clearly the priority of the women in the announcement of the Resurrection, and we may add a second condition to the first that we set: In order to understand this announcement, it is not enough to touch a dead body, it is necessary also to be ready to carry a living one (without which death cannot reach you in your inner depths). And to be ready to carry a living body is to have gone through the fundamental question, the one underlying the very possibility of the human adventure: Why bother to give life if ultimately it is so that this life can be annihilated? What good is it to have children if there is no resurrection, but only dust—dust over which you cannot even run the vacuum cleaner?

Here again we have our main thesis: a miracle is not there to make us experience extraordinary things, but rather so that we might live the most ordinary things in an extraordinary way. Now, among the most ordinary things there is this one, which is already extraordinary for a man: being a woman. Why the feminine? The masculine can be understood: it is a body full of itself, that makes things with its hands outside of itself. But the feminine is a body that is naturally surrendered, with its hollow in the middle, a hollow inside of which is engendered, as we said, not something but someone, obscurely, without needing one's hands. Why consent to this surrendered body? Why a womb if ultimately its fruit must rot in a pine box (for the Christmas tree is sawed up into planks for a coffin)? But here is why: Jesus is risen from the tomb, and man and woman can sleep together. They can share a bed, without fearing the creation of a new little mortal—for it is no longer in vain—and with sufficient love to lie down, still beside one another, in the same vault.

Fear of the resurrection

There is cause to fear. The resurrection is very troubling not only for the owners of funeral parlors, but also for merry widows who have remarried, heirs who are dividing up the loot, or assassins who have managed to turn over a new leaf. When Herod heard of the cures performed by Jesus, there he was, *perplexed, because it was said by some that John had been raised from the dead* (Lk 9:7). We can sympathize with his uneasiness. If the dead can be raised up, there is good reason to be perplexed. It is not very pleasant to run into someone on the street whom you had made sure to behead the day before yesterday—and who greets you by doffing his head along with his hat.

More generally, faith in the resurrection happens to destroy two contrary beliefs, each of which is rather convenient on its own terms: the belief in the immortality of the soul alone, and the belief in death as total annihilation. Annihilation allows you to bury with you all your unknown crimes. Exclusively spiritual immortality allows you to disdain the body in this world and to accept death as a release from prison. These two ways out are now impossible. In order to be a good resurrected person, it is necessary first to have died well (by a death that is still scandalous). But, in order to die well it is necessary first to live well. Herod sensed this: if one does not live well here and now, if one does not already love one's neighbor, there is the risk that a general resurrection would go rather badly for a conscientious exterminator, since he would then be obliged to stand side by side with his glorious victim (but the event would be even more painful for the rich, haughty philanthropist, condemned now actually to meet poor people who no longer need his money). Hence this lukewarm advice from the prophet Daniel (12:2): *Many of those who sleep in the dust of the earth shall awake, some to everlasting life, and some to shame and everlasting contempt.*

But there is something more. If Jesus comes back in his body and lives among us, it is perhaps because it is rather good to live in a body and to walk the earth. Until now, the women could only be mourners. They could defer the moment of joy to another world. They could tell themselves that things would only be all right somewhere else, far from everyday routine, far from the housekeeping, in a future without wombs, where everything runs smoothly. And suddenly, instead of departing directly for heaven, the Lord is there, he lingers, he once again uses everyday words and will even do a bit of cooking on a wood fire.

III

THE

HEAD-CLOTH

IN ITS PLACE

Now on the first day of the week, Mary Magdalene came to the tomb early, while it was still dark, and saw that the stone had been taken away from the tomb. So she ran, and went to Simon Peter and the other disciple, the one whom Jesus loved, and said to them, "They have taken the Lord out of the tomb, and we do not know where they have laid him." Peter than came out with the other disciple, and they went toward the tomb. They both ran, but the other disciple outran Peter and reached the tomb first; and stooping to look in, he saw the linen cloths lying there, but he did not go in. Then Simon Peter came, following him, and went into the tomb; he saw the linen cloths lying, and the napkin, which had been on his head, not lying with the linen cloths but rolled up in a place by itself. Then the other disciple, who reached the tomb first, also went in, and he saw and believed.

John 20:1-8

I know people who go jogging on the weekend. They are so admirable, so swift, so regular in their stride that, in comparison, my wife and I, with our six children gesticulating every which way as we plod slowly on, resemble two big jars of jelly surrounded by a cloud of gnats. What are they looking for, those Sunday runners? Fitness. To have their heart and body in good shape. And they are quite right. The only little minor problem is that all of them, in spite of it all, are also running toward their grave. Which would still be no big thing except for the other problem that some people tend to forget: that their heart is not only a muscle.

Far be it from me, in any case, to disdain them. If we are to believe Saint John, on Easter Sunday, everyone started running. The verb "to run" is even reserved in his Gospel for that day, for the comings and goings at the tomb. Here we see first of all that woman—everybody knows her, an old sinner!—who runs through the streets of Jerusalem and shoves you as she passes: "Really, young woman, you could pay more attention!" And, suddenly, here we have two men—everybody knows them, fishermen on early retirement!—who are running in the opposite direction and bump into you once again: "What has got into them all today? Grief over your master ought to sink you into motionless somberness and mourning! Do you have so little feeling?" This is the reproach that a good Christian would not hesitate to level at the

Apostles, especially if he himself strives at Mass to be as warm and lively as a marble statue.

Apparently, if we were to redesign the ritual according to the Paschal behavior of Peter, John, and Mary Magdalene, we would have to organize something as incongruous as relay races around the altar, and reenergize the congregation with each lap by rereading this passage from the First Letter of Paul to the Corinthians: *Do you not know that in a race all the runners compete, but only one receives the prize? So run that you may obtain it* (1 Cor 9:24).

"After you"

The impressive thing here is that John, with his young legs, arrives at the tomb sooner than Peter, but he stops at the threshold and lets the older man go ahead. He could very well not have waited for him. Considering the exceptional circumstances, haste was called for: someone had *taken the Lord* away; such a theft is an emergency that quite legitimately suspends the ordinary rules of decorum. John, however, does not see it that way. He is a perfect gentleman. The kind of guy who on an airplane in distress still offers to carry an old man's baggage upon arrival, or reassures a young woman that her life jacket suits her stunningly. And it is as if the mystery of the Resurrection had the purpose of teaching us to practice in all circumstances this sort of exquisite thoughtfulness.

Some will observe that in this gesture of letting Peter go in first lies proof of his primacy in the college of Apostles and, therefore, an affirmation of the papacy in the Church. And they will be right. But this does not stop us from seeing in it a particular example of a more general rule: that of letting an older person have your seat on a bus, because even though we can run faster, we should recognize that that person nevertheless has taken more steps than we have. Though we can also do this for a person who is younger—for a woman, perhaps, if one is a man—simply because that person is someone *else*. Thus the French philosopher Emmanuel Lévinas asserted that the finest definition of civilization was encapsulated in this well-mannered formula: "After you." If the pope goes first, this is an eminent way of applying the definition by making himself "the servant of the servants of God"; and this is why it is good to have sovereigns and kings: to offer us striking examples of humility. Louis the Pious signed charters with a title that abdicated all distinctions, even to lowliness: "Our Mediocrity." Egalitarianism can only preclude such examples as these: when you put everyone on the same level, no one can humble himself any more, no one can really elevate himself either, and ultimately everyone is dragged into unfair competition—for loyalty remains based on hierarchy.

But why this "After you"? Isn't there something suspicious about it? Isn't it about self-denial? How can love of neighbor be founded upon hatred of self? Unless this is like a bank shot in billiards. We visibly abase ourselves, the better to ascend in the estimation of those looking on; we put ourselves in the last place, *so that when your host comes he may say to you, 'Friend, go up higher'* (Lk 14:10). Finally, if everyone says to his neighbor, "After you," we risk causing traffic jams in the waiting lines at the Department of Motor Vehicles, even if clerks are available. . . . We see this sort of dysfunctional behavior in Kafka: two executioners incessantly give each other the honor of killing a condemned criminal. They hand each other the ax back and forth and, through their polite manners, postpone the execution indefinitely.

A miracle in the hollow

If John is self-effacing with regard to Peter, it is so that Peter might be spectator to another act of self-effacement: that of Jesus' body. *He saw the linen cloths lying* [a more literal translation would read *strips of cloth*], *and the napkin, which had been on his head, not lying with the strips of cloth but rolled up in a place by itself* (Jn 20:6-7). The tomb is empty, but it is even more astonishing that it is not entirely empty. The shroud is still there. And it is rolled up as at the hour of the burial, except that now the envelope has collapsed upon the divine absence. If there had been a theft, they would have taken the body with its wrappings, or they would have undone the wrappings and taken only the body, or else they would have taken the body and left the wrappings folded with a solicitude that scarcely befits a thief—but in any case they would not have been able to roll it up again to fit the dimensions of the body. The exploit outdoes Houdini himself. Peter is very cautious, however, not to draw hasty conclusions from this. He exhibits the circumspection worthy of a pope.

John, who enters after him, will take the lead again, not spatially, but in faith (as though Peter had returned to him, in the spiritual order, the "After you" that had been granted to him in the material order). *He saw and believed* (Jn 20:8). What did he see, then, to believe suddenly, the first of all, that Christ was risen? Very precisely: nothing. He saw nothing. Or rather he saw the strips of cloth that had collapsed onto themselves, and through this chrysalis that had been vacated without being torn, the conspicuous effacement of his Master.

The miracle of miracles is a concave miracle—as every true miracle ought to be, incidentally. It "makes room," as we said earlier, and thereby prolongs the Shabbat. If the Risen One had turned up with flashes of lightning and peals of thunder, amid hosts of angels, he would be scarcely distinguishable from the attention-seekers who have themselves announced amid great trumpet blasts. He has no need to impress anyone. On the contrary, he effaces himself; with his body he performs the eternal "After you."

Like a mother

And I do mean he "effaces" himself, and not he "absents" or "withdraws" himself. For truly he is still there. And more present than when he was visible. The only person who can say to us, "After you" is someone who was there *previously*. The space that he frees up is ours only because it was first his own.

Some, prompted by the insight into this "After you," imagine that, in order to create the world, God had to withdraw as the sea turns back and uncovers the shore, or as an elephant steps aside a bit to avoid crushing the ant. These pretty images unfortunately present to us a Creator who is situated on the same level as his creation and, therefore, in competition with it: he must diminish so that it might increase. Then too, the image can be twisted around to become one of the principles of atheism: we will have to kill the elephant and take its ivory, drain the ocean and reclaim more land to have a maximum of inhabitable surface area. In other words, for creation to take full flight, it will be necessary to annihilate the Creator entirely. But when God makes room, he actually *makes* that room. He does not clear it, as though something was there before his action; he gives it being in that same action: if he is a sea that withdraws, then he is a sea that simultaneously constitutes the earth down to its elementary particles; and if he is an elephant who steps aside, then he is an elephant who in fact engenders both the ant and the space-time that circumscribes its existence.

There is one analogy that combines effacement and envelopment at the same time, complete invisibility and total presence—a withdrawal without retreat in which the hollow is not emptiness but like the hollow of the hand, the fullness of tenderness and nourishment. It is the analogy of the maternal womb. The Hebrew name for it in the Bible—*Rahamim*—also means "mercy." In pregnancy, the mother makes room but does not draw back like the sea. For she makes room in her own body, by nourishing with her own body the child for whom she makes room, by surrounding him entirely with her warmth, by carrying him in his invisible presence.

This is the sense in which "After you" can designate even the Creator's act, the result neither of self-denial nor indirect self-exaltation, but from an affirmation that is broad and discreet as well. Look: you do not see him, and this is precisely because he creates you, you and everything around you. As the very principle of one who makes space for the other, his apparent absence is his generous presence: After you, heaven and earth! After you, sun, moon, and all the constellations! After you, birds, fish, and everything that creeps and walks and runs on the ground! After you, man, and woman, and child!

God does not need to put himself in the spotlight and say: "Let me be!" He says: "Let there be light," and the light arrives within his Word. Unceasingly, the Creator does not step aside but advances to allow us too to go forward (as the belly of a pregnant woman precedes her like a prow). He envelops us so thoroughly that we almost have good reason to think that he does not exist (and, in fact, he does not exist in the same way as creatures do). The fetus does not see his mother; and if he can think that he has no mother, it is just because everything is a *sign* of her presence, because she is present *everywhere*—and not only *somewhere* inside her belly. The atheist belief is still an unconscious homage rendered to the immeasurable goodness of the eternal One.

Housekeeping

Not only was there the shroud, intact and collapsed flatter than a cheese soufflé. There was also the face-cloth, set aside. Some exegetes read this verse to mean that the *sudarium*, or sweat-cloth, that covered the Holy Face was not folded and set aside, outside the strips of cloth, but that it remained inside the shroud, at face level. It seems to me that this interpretation, like some very lofty symbolic interpretations, serves to provide an excellent excuse for not helping with the household chores. It leaves us at the wondrous disappearance, without thinking of what is even still more woundrous, namely, that the first thing the Risen Lord did was to fold and carefully arrange his face-cloth like a napkin after dinner. Maybe that was the sign that overwhelmed John: Christ began his glorified life by performing the simple act of a washerwoman.

You will probably say that I'm exaggerating. Some want everything to amount to the coarseness of grand spectacle, or a demonstration of power. This is because they probably have not advanced far enough into the mysticism of housekeeping. For what is more in the image of God, along the lines that we have just seen, than keeping house? *I will sweep away the house of Jeroboam, as a man sweeps away dung until it is all gone*, says the Lord through the mouth of the prophet Ahijah (1 Kgs 14:10). And Jesus *clears his threshing floor* (cf. Mt 3:12), drives the merchants out of the Temple, and washes the feet of his disciples. (We might think here of a curling player as opposed to a hockey player: the hockey player drives the puck by hitting it with the stick, while the curling player sweeps the ice in front of the stone, which then glides effortlessly toward the goal, as though under its own impetus.)

A true manager is closer to a housewife than to a little corporal. She rarely "takes center stage," yet thanks to her there is a welcoming scene where the "actors" can play. She does not wear their colorful costumes, but she washed, pressed, and mended them and put them on hangers in their dressing room. Hence that pervasive sweetness in a home: when the laundry is in its place, when the parquet floor shines, when the table is set and the aroma from the simmering dish tickles your nostrils, when your clothes are clean and the color and fabric of the curtains and the sofas have been chosen with flawless taste; in short, when every corner of the house shows signs of delicate attentions that change a square box into a home where it is good to live and to converse. . . . Isn't this a perfect imitation of God, *who formed the earth and made it; he established it; he did not create it a chaos, he formed it to be inhabited* (Is 45:18)?

Thus, at the beginning and at the end of the cycle of his apparitions, in the discovery of his absence at the tomb as well as in the vision of his Ascension on the Mount of Olives, the Risen One effaces himself before his disciples, and he effaces himself because he goes to *prepare a place* for them and, afterward, another coming (Jn 14:3). John sees this vacant place calling him; in it he hears the most discreet and most intimate "After you" (which is another way of saying, "It's your turn"), and he believes.

P.S. To my wife: Darling, I spoke this way about housekeeping, not so that you might apply yourself to it more assiduously, outdoing the depressing cliché of the submissive wife. It's metaphysics. I can't help it. Besides, you must acknowledge that by this meditation I have deprived myself of my best excuses.

IV
GO DOWN AND
SEE IF I'M THERE

Mary stood weeping outside the tomb, and as she wept she stooped to look into the tomb; and she saw two angels in white, sitting where the body of Jesus had lain, one at the head and one at the feet. They said to her, "Woman, why are you weeping?" She said to them, "Because they have taken away my Lord, and I do not know where they have laid him." Saying this, she turned round and saw Jesus standing, but she did not know that it was Jesus. Jesus said to her, "Woman, why are you weeping? Whom do you seek?" Supposing him to be the gardener, she said to him, "Sir, if you have carried him away, tell me where you have laid him, and I will take him away." Jesus said to her, "Mary." She turned and said to him in Hebrew, "Rabboni!" (which means Teacher). Jesus said to her, "Do not hold me, for I have not yet ascended to the Father; but go to my brethren and say to them, I am ascending to my Father and your Father, to my God and your God." Mary Magdalene went and said to the disciples, "I have seen the Lord"; and she told them that he had said these things to her.

John 20:11-18

It is quite possible to read the Gospel as a police investigation, as long you realize its structure is more surprising than an Agatha Christie mystery, or even Sophocles' *Oedipus Rex*. In the famous Greek tragedy, Oedipus conducts the investigation and, at its conclusion, discovers that the criminal is none other than the detective, that is, himself. The reader, however, is still innocent and is spared—at least until the psychoanalyst arrives and tries to persuade him that he too is Oedipus. The Gospel does not need to resort to Freudian strategies. It is enough to read it—and not even between the lines—to perceive that *Christ died for our sins in accordance with the Scriptures* (1 Cor 15:3), and that, consequently, behind Pilate, the crowd of Jews, and the high priests, there is me (which is to say you, too, dear reader), and that they were for us like so many instruments or devoted collaborators.

But the investigation does not stop there. There is a second part to it, which does not seem to fall within the province of any police service that existed in those days, even though some are sure to think that the crime and anti-narcotics squad could tackle it together. In any case, if such a squad came into being, its patron saint would be Mary Magdalene. She in particular is the one who carries the second part of the affair: the mystery of the empty tomb, which is much more mysterious than a locked-room mystery such as Agatha Christie's *And Then There Were None*. For after the murder case, which is quickly solved (it was me that did it—meaning you, too, dear reader), comes the Resurrection, an occurrence that is so rare as to disconcert both Sherlock Holmes and Hercule Poirot. And its enigma is this: Where is Christ's body now?

Understand that this is a question not only of seeing him again after discovering the empty tomb, but of knowing where he resides at present, after the Ascension. Is it among the stars, between the constellations Ursa Major and Leo Minor? Or rather in the tabernacle of the neighborhood church? The Creed declares, without any political connotation, that he is on the right—at the right hand of the Father. But where is that, this right hand that is not mine might just as well be my left?

Non-recognition

At first glance, Mary Magdalene is no Miss Marple. She walks right past the most obvious clues. First of all, she sees and hears two angels—and this awakens not the slightest suspicion in her: the celestial creatures do not hold her attention any more than two walk-on actors in the background of the great love scene. Then, when she ought to immediately proceed to a proper interrogation in due form to find her first lead, she remains silent and allows herself to be interrogated: *Woman, why are you weeping?* The angels are plainly more interested in her than she is in them. Finally, when Jesus appears and she runs smack into the man whom she is looking for, instead of recognizing him right away, she mistakes him for the local gardener, or·worse yet—for the Number One suspect: *Sir, if you have carried him away, tell me where you have laid him*. It does happen, though, that by dint of somersaults one lands like a cat on all fours. And that is the case here. Mary Magdalene was so wrong about the direction that the sum total of all her deviations leads her to the right path. She has good reason to suppose that she is face to face with the abductor: it is indeed he—even though she has not yet grasped the fact that the abductor and the one carried off are one and the same.

How are we to interpret this blindness? Is Mary Magdalene the one at fault, or is it her interlocutors who deliberately disorient her with their calculated disguise? Why do the angels show themselves with so few identifying marks (wings and halos) that they can be mistaken for any old guys? And above all, why did Christ make himself unrecognizable to the point of appearing to be the prime suspect to the woman who had been so close to him? He could very easily have made sure that Mary Magdalene or the disciples on the road to Emmaus would identify him instantly. He deliberately preferred to play hide-and-seek. Now that all the gravity of the cross has been passed through, Wisdom *plays on the surface of the earth, and his delights are to be with the children of men* (cf. Prv 8:31, Vulgate).

Transmitting the untranslatable

And then Jesus calls her by name: "Mariam!" and the Magdalene suddenly recovers herself and her memories: "Rabboni!" she exclaims, her eyes now opened by her ears. This is the only dialogue that the Evangelist decided to preserve in Hebrew. Why all of a sudden this "local color"? It is for exotic effect? More likely for the sake of emphasis. This face-to-face conversation must not be reported in Greek. It has to be set apart; its untranslatable singularity must be preserved, to recall that there is something irreplaceable about a true encounter.

This brief dialogue sums up in itself all the words that two lovers exchange, which cannot help but sound hollow to an outsider—hollow and silly and of no use whatsoever in advancing our knowledge. What matters between lovers is not the information (otherwise what good is it to repeat "I love you"?), it is not the content ("I love you" explains nothing to us, and may even appear quite presumptuous), nor is it the form (saying it in a very beautiful poem is not more beautiful, and can even lead to becoming too fond of the sound of one's own voice), but rather it is a particular quality of the tone, the fact that this "I love you," which cannot be taken for granted, is addressed to you, to you alone, to the point where the lover may not say it but only repeat your name: "Maria," as in *West Side Story*: "All the beautiful sounds of the world in a single word. . . / Say it loud and there's music playing; / Say it soft and it's almost like praying. . . ."

John thereby teaches us something that cannot just remain the object of general teaching (there is a well-known maxim of Zhuang Zhou that French author Paul Claudel wanted to have engraved on the pediment of every school: "What is worth the trouble to learn cannot be taught.") Mary does not reply "My beloved"; she replies "Master." A master is always more than a teacher: with him, the auditorium becomes an Upper Room, the professorial discourse is surpassed by the call to carry on. Beneath the words, we enter into something so intimate and unique, that firstly concerns me personally—something no one else could hear in my place. The student turns into a witness: no longer is it the content of the lesson alone that must be transmitted, but the master's countenance, his way of life, and for that there is no other option than to enter into this way of life—following him—as original as that may be.

True glory does not consist of being immediately recognizable by one's sequined gown, one's name in neon lights, one's appearance just like on the billboard: "It's him! The guy in the film by Mel Gibson and also in the CBS series *Person of Interest*!" What happens in this sort of vainglory is precisely the opposite of what is claimed: the star's image becomes more important than the star himself, and identifying him relates now only to that commercialized image. . . . Mary does not recognize Jesus by his famous face or even by his voice. She recognizes him by her vocation. What matters is not an external, common image, but an interior, personal echo. He calls her by her own name and entrusts to her the task of transmitting to the others her testimony of this incommunicable face-to-face encounter. And this is why the others, to begin with, cannot bring themselves to believe her. The Good News escapes the parameters of news: it is not information for everyone, but a call to each.

Return from Eden

The symmetry between the Fall in Eden and this restoration in the garden has often been emphasized. There, the innocent woman succumbed to the serpent's temptation and gave the forbidden fruit to Adam. Here, the sinful woman is surprised by the Savior's Resurrection and brings the announcement of this miracle to her brethren. Mark's text captures the event in a single shocking sentence in which the immediacy experienced by Mary Magdalene collides with the corruption in which she had found herself not long before: *When he rose early on the first day of the week, he appeared first to Mary Magdalene, from whom he had cast out seven demons* (Mk 16:9).

The supernatural springtime is manifested in the first place to the faded flower—to *the woman* who had had a demon for each day of the week or one to oppose each gift of the Holy Spirit: the demon of fear of events, with its fur bristling in anticipation of a caress; the demon of worldly piety, which lifts itself up by creeping like ivy; the demon of proud science, hiding its horns beneath a university mortarboard; the demon of quick-tempered strength that is incapable of enduring the least vexation; the demon of bad counsel, that tells you all the tricks by which to climb the rungs of hell; the demon of artificial intelligence, that believes that thought is perfected not in praise but in calculation; the demon of the wisdom of spirituality websites, which provide you with "well-being, interior freedom, harmony, and serenity in everyday life" by assuring you that you are the reincarnation of an empress and that your boss is only an illusion. Our Mary, who is neither a saint nor a virgin, had all it would take to succeed in high society. No such luck, or perhaps by the grace of God, whichever you prefer: there she was, deprived of the seven keys to success and commanded by the Risen Lord to relate an impossible story to a bunch of dullards.

To the serpent, *the woman* had said that they must not eat or touch the fruit of the tree in the middle of the garden, but this was incorrect: the Lord had never forbidden them to touch it. Now, just the opposite, the first commandment that Jesus gives to the one whom the angels and he himself at first called *Woman* is: *Do not touch me*. Was it, as some prudes think, to thwart an excessively sensual embrace on the part of the former prostitute? That interpretation overlooks the fact that—again an analogy with Eden—although Jesus forbids her to touch him, he commands her to go and tell her brethren. The debauchee turns into an apostle: yesterday, the woman communicated the lie to the man; today, Mary must proclaim the Risen Lord to men. And, by symmetry, whereas the forbidden fruit could be touched but not eaten, Jesus, who is also the *living* Bread (Jn 6:51), must not be touched but may be eaten. The one who says *Do not touch me* is in fact the same one who said a few verses earlier: *Unless you eat the flesh of the Son of man and drink his blood, you have no life in you* (Jn 6:53). His *Noli me tangere* is thus coupled with the recommendation to take him into a wide-open mouth, more savagely than in the most ardent kiss, in other words, to receive him in the Eucharist. The interpretation therefore requires a bit more tact. It brings us back, incidentally, to the enigma of our police investigation.

The problem of the Incarnation

Where is the body of the Risen One? Is it simply here, before Mary Magdalene, one body among others? But then why his Resurrection, if it changes nothing of his condition before death? Maybe our detective did have more flair than Miss Marple, when all is said and done. Maybe she was not entirely wrong not to recognize him, to mistake him for a municipal gardener or even for a grave robber.

The Incarnation has always been a problem from the perspective of the Jews. To them it seems to contradict love of neighbor. By plunging divine transcendence into the immanence of this world, it appears to degrade it in a way that we denounced earlier: the competition of the Creator with the creature, the competition of the Son with the brother. As long as the eternal One is not a man but the author of all things, I can encounter him only through each human being (and even each mosquito), just as we know a great author only through his books or his correspondence. But if he becomes this man here, then I will have the tendency to turn toward him and no longer see that man there, my neighbor, whom I've always disliked anyway. Frank and Michelle are here, but now God comes into the room with more dignity than John Wayne entering the saloon. Other poor saps pale in comparison. And then I will not miss an opportunity to "contemplate Jesus," especially since it gives me a good reason to turn away from Frank or Michelle. The same problem has repercussions in dealing with images: why pray in front of an icon of Jesus and not in front of one's child, one's wife, one's father-in-law, the plumber, the homeless man, or even a member of the House Budget Committee? Not only does the body of Christ tend to eclipse the body of Frank, but even the icon of

Christ tends to make us forget that Frank is in the image of Elohim, more than any depiction, even though his company is about as welcome as an asthma attack. Doesn't the Incarnation, with the iconography it authorizes, cause us to backslide into idolatry? For idolatry, in its worst aspects, is nothing other than despising one's neighbor. Formally, it consists of rendering to a creature the honor due to the Creator, but the immediate consequence of the honor granted to this privileged creature is the ability to exclude absolutely all the other creatures from our field of attention. This exclusion is what motivates idolatry, which would be inexplicable without it. Ultimately, we are justified in turning away all these importunate people, especially Frank and Michelle! Get out of here, you pathetic lot! I have to welcome the Lord who is passing by!

To open our eyes

It is appropriate nonetheless to offer a little reminder, which is naïve yet indisputable: a portrait can teach us to better appreciate the mugs surrounding us. Because I admired at the Louvre this canvas by Domenico Ghirlandaio of an old man with a big pimply nose, I can now see in a big pimply nose a masterpiece. Some Cubist pictures have even managed to make me realize that there could be something of interest in Frank's conversation.

Our intellect is so weak that it needs examples. Including examples for the simplest things, as we already remarked. When a bartender pours me a beer, I'm not ecstatic, but if the king is the one who pours me that same beer: "What goodness! What admirable condescension!" That God should become human, that he should espouse our everyday actions and thereby reconnect them with their sacred source—this seems necessary, not in order to accomplish unheard-of exploits, but in order to save the most elementary gestures: pouring a beer, chopping some wood, walking with friends, sharing a bit of bread, sweetly calling my wife—"Siffreine"—by her name, just as Jesus said "Mary"—without immediately throwing myself at her. . . .

Valentinus the Gnostic rejected the reality of the Incarnation because he thought it undignified of the Word of God to go to the bathroom. But to think that the Word of God went to the bathroom is part of a more transcendent mysticism: it transforms our rest rooms into places conducive to the most profound contemplation (we will return to this in the next chapter). Here Christianity goes further than paganism in its most beautiful aspects. Paganism sees a dryad behind a tree, a water nymph hidden in a spring, etc. These little agrarian and woodland deities imbue the wheat, the olive tree, the bowl, and the plow with the poetry we find in the writings of Virgil and Ovid. But to say that God himself, in his undiminished transcendence, came to share our everyday life by becoming a laborer in Nazareth? A carpenter's plane becomes a divine instrument. The simplest stroll down a street becomes a mission from on high. Eating a fig and drinking some water are transformed into such messianic acts that it is necessary to fast sometimes in order to approach the mystery more worthily. Breathing suddenly appears to be a breathtaking event. And speaking with one's mother, working with sinners (Peter, James, John. . .) or tax collectors (Matthew, Zacchaeus), conversing with a woman who has been divorced seven times (the Samaritan)—from now on all this is on the order of the loftiest spirituality.

The largest in the smallest

In becoming one of us, the Son does not steal our spotlight; I repeat, he prepares a divine place for us. And this is why, at the end of his earthly career, the body of the Risen One is no longer to be sought as one body among others, but as the body of which all other bodies are very really members: *Now you are the body of Christ and individually members of it. . . . We are members one of another* (1 Cor 12:27 and Eph 4:25).

This is the end of the investigation, the answer to the riddle the body of Christ is to be found in the body of my neighbor. And my neighbor is perhaps a knee while I am an armpit, or the forearm while I am the calf. The finger of God? That's the guy who's just stepped on your toes. I admit that you have to have faith to recognize him. But this is where the encounter in the garden accomplishes the return from the Fall: the serpent's lie, *You will be like gods*, becomes Christ's truth. And this is where our investigation should ultimately lead: If you want to find the body of the Risen One, *go to his brethren*.

This explains why Jesus showed himself to Mary Magdalene and not to Mary of Nazareth. It is not so much because he was seeking to avoid the inevitable solicitude of a Jewish mother: "Do they feed you well down there? And the descent into hell, I hope it wasn't too rough. . . . Let me straighten your white garment a bit. . . . As a matter of fact, she did not even need to see the collapsed winding cloths in order to believe. She knew that the one for whom she had made room in her womb was there to prepare a shining place for each of us. She had heard him say: *As you did it to one of the least of these my brethren, you did it to me* (Mt 25:40). She was already seeing the body of her risen Son in the least, in the dullest—and even in the most brilliant (the guy who needs to *make* himself interesting because he does not think that he is, and who therefore is atrociously petty—I know something about that—and even in that guy Mary can see her child).

V

DO YOU HAVE SOMETHING TO EAT?

When he was at table with them, he took the bread and blessed and broke it, and gave it to them. And their eyes were opened and they recognized him; and he vanished out of their sight. . . . And while they still disbelieved for joy, and wondered, he said to them, "Have you anything here to eat?"

Luke 24:30-31, 41

When they got out on land, they saw a charcoal fire there, with fish lying on it, and bread. . . . Jesus said to them, "Come and have breakfast." Now none of the disciples dared ask him, "Who are you?" They knew it was the Lord. Jesus came and took the bread and gave it to them, and so with the fish.

John 21:9, 12-13

And while eating with them. . . .

Acts 1:4

"Our digestions, for instance, going sacredly and silently right, that is the foundation of all poetry." This statement by G. K. Chesterton may seem very prosaic. It is entirely in keeping with the Resurrection.

In his glorified state, Jesus does not need to eat. And yet he does. Why? He had resisted Satan by recalling the words of Deuteronomy (8:3): *Man shall not live by bread alone, but by every word that proceeds from the mouth of God* (Mt 4:4); why then, at the very moment when he can live by the mouth of God alone, did he decide to keep feeding himself with bread? Many say that it was to prove that he was not a ghost but had a real body of certifiable flesh. Someone who stops at that is only one step away from thinking that Jesus is pretending. And when heartburn arrives it is easy to take that step: no, Jesus takes no pleasure in these meals, and he certainly does not digest (for fear that his digestion is not glorious enough to leave no waste), so that, despite their initial affirmation, he must be a ghost after all, the only difference being that he is more clever than other ghosts at producing illusions.

For my part, I am rather reluctant to think that the Truth could lie. If he did not pretend to have a body, he could not pretend to eat. When the Truth shares a meal with his disciples, he truly shares it. No doubt in doing so he makes the theologians' task no easier. At least he glorifies the task of those who eat, who for the moment are a little more numerous (whatever they may think, the theologians themselves are part of the latter group). And he confirms Chesterton's insight: since the Risen One does not eat out of want, he can do so only for the sake of poetry. This fundamental poetry is the present topic for meditation.

Beauty secret

Of course there is *destruction* for those whose *god is the belly* (Phil 3:19). But that is because these gluttonous idolaters have not sufficiently reflected on the divine aspects of their belly. Had they done so, they would most certainly have purified their appetite. If you reflect just for a moment on this orchestration of such varied organs, from the incisors to the rear end, with the miracle of the sphincter muscles and peristalsis, the two hundred million neurons decentralized in our intestines, the allied action of enzymes and bacteria in symbiosis (there are one hundred times as many of these bacteria in each of us as there are of our own cells, and under our belts they make up the most dense ecosystem on the planet!), the delicate absorption of nutrients by the small intestine and the colon, that pipeline that is twice as long as a boa constrictor, not to mention the saliva that comes to wet your whistle through your eyes or through the sense of smell or through the imagination (picture your favorite dish and feel the flood invading your mouth), and the stupefying stomach that secretes liters of hydrochloric acid and at the same time the mucus that enables it not to devour itself! What more admirable mechanism is there? What machine is capable of this process that derives energy and building materials, not from fuel, but from food?

A fuel or energy source (natural gas, gasoline, electricity) simply makes a machine run. When you don't supply it, the machine continues to exist. It has stopped, but it does not die. The fuel does not reconstitute. It does not keep the motor in existence, nor the chassis, nor any other piece whatsoever of the automobile. Food, in contrast, not only furnishes the calories that enable the body to function; more fundamentally it contributes to the subsistence, the growth, and then even the fecundity of the individual whom it nourishes. This is expressed in the etymology of the incredible words "restaurant" (French: restoring) and "refectory" (Latin: place for remaking). In eating, we restore ourselves, we remake and regenerate ourselves (not to say "resuscitate ourselves").

What happens when a stuffed turkey is consumed by the beautiful Gisele Bündchen? It is turned into the very substance of the top model, whose body mass, sinuous curves, and graceful stride on the catwalk benefited yesterday also from a dish of mussels, a broccoli quiche, and who knows what else? Some quinoa-tofu served with Bordeaux: all the foodstuffs of the world have passed through that convoluted still, distilling more than ambrosia! The greatest contemporary artist cannot hold a candle to the digestive system. He cannot combine to such a vivid degree the horrific and the splendid. He could never manage to turn steak and potatoes so subtly into the radiant form of a woman.

Dependence and assumption

This assimilation process has often been reduced to a metaphor for greed: someone who eats reduces everything to himself. But as soon as you consider it a bit more closely, it appears instead as an exhortation to the utmost modesty: even the most spiritual man still depends on the whiff of oxygen, the bowl of soup, the slice of bread. Without something to eat, our fine autonomy wastes away. We don't feel right if we don't eat right. We stay standing with the support of the air: if air is lacking, we collapse. We walk on the ground by walking on water: if water is lacking, we dry up on the spot. Do not ask the poet to intone his sublime song if he has not had a chance to bite into his bread and butter, or sip his coffee. The Muse is his inspiration, but Grub is his refreshment. If he is to live on his verses, his verses have to procure him some vittles.

May he become aware of this, and may this dependence lead him to gratitude. "Hail to the chicken thigh without which I could no longer stand on my own two feet! Thanks be to the lettuce without which I could not turn over a new leaf to write again! Hosanna to the breath of fresh air, without which my lips would be incapable of praise!" The primitive act of nutrition causes all these things to be transformed into my words and, so that my words might assimilate them completely, invites me to offer to them in return a spiritual legacy and moral respect. The air becomes the air of a song, an *aria*; the lettuce ushers in the salad days of my writing career, and the chicken is metamorphosed into such a beautiful symbol that Jesus likens himself to *a hen [that] gathers her brood under her wings* (Mt 23:37). And so I can no longer treat them any old way. Their edible presence is a primordial gift that I must take good care of, which invites me to gratitude. The rumblings in my gut tell me about it. They constitute the first phrases of a harmony that I must continue. For how does it happen that there are edible things? Whence this compatibility between my body and the world? Hunters and gatherers are convinced that there is something divine about the reindeer and the wild strawberry. This conviction is more rare in the customer at the supermarket. The packaging might lead him to believe that everything grows right there in the display cases of the Shop Rite (a substitute for Providence). If he can suppose that he is the master and owner of nature, it is because nature first offers itself to his grasp. But man is not the author of this first offering of nature, nor of his ability to accept it or take it. Dyspeptics will no doubt find some fault in it, and so will gluttons. The former feel resentment toward food, because they digest it poorly; the latter do not have the time to savor it with their mind, because they swallow it too quickly. Both groups can exclaim: "Celebrating the chicken thigh, the poultry farmer, and the Creator in the same hymn! Claiming to accompany it with the chords of digestion! Such poetry is certainly eccentric and crazy!" It is one of the most common types of verse. The poetry of blessings, graces, and thanksgivings. And this is the ultimate meaning of physiology.

Christ reminds his Apostles of this. After his Resurrection, his body now continues to exist through the life that he draws from his eternal source. If he eats again, it is therefore not out of dependency but by way of assumption. He assumes our ordinary routine into his glory, so that we might recognize in our ordinary routine a marvelous order and understand that the bread itself proceeds from the mouth of God. When Saint Paul exhorts his Christian brethren: *Whether you eat or drink, or whatever you do, do all to the glory of God* (1 Cor 10:31), he is not issuing an external command, according to a devotion superimposed on digestion. He is proclaiming a devotion that flourishes on the basis of digestion itself. He is just asking Christians to be lucid, to notice what is already there, to consider that eating and drinking are in themselves amazing operations, and therefore, to use an expression that is not altogether exaggerated, to follow our gut feeling about them.

The law of the table

In the Gospel, our Lord distributes loaves and fishes miraculously on several occasions, but we have to wait until his Resurrection for him to simply start cooking. It would take an event of that magnitude to get some married men (acquaintances of mine) to stand in front of a stove—and sometimes their wives, too, so mesmerized are some by the abundance of frozen meals today. Therefore all is not hopeless. The Risen One builds a fire on the shore and places some fish and bread on it. What?! Jesus delivered us from hell to teach us how to improvise a barbecue? The Gospel concludes with a recipe for grilled tilapia? Golgotha was meant to lead to the revelation of the picnic? The Word descended from heaven, rose again from hell, and all this just to call, like any mother of a family, "Come, children: dinnertime!"

I discovered in an interview with Marguerite Duras a remark that may shed light for us on this mystery of simplicity: "Never in any case," she says, "should you cook for yourself alone. Because I think that that is the path that leads to despair as a permanent fixture. To make home-fried potatoes or a Vietnamese omelet for yourself is literally unthinkable. Food is truly made for everybody. Like life, it is truly made for all. Literature is not."

A meal is at the same time less abstract and more universal than words and ideas. At the opening of an exhibition, agreement is more unanimous around the buffet than in front of the works of art. Only a few people can meet at an exhibition or a conference: it depends on their aesthetic affinities, their political commitments, their intellectual orientations. Everyone meets around a table: it requires no other qualification than being hungry. There the learned and the ignorant meet, the old man and the child, the rich and the poor, the innocent and the sinner, the sophisticate and the pain-in-the-neck, and finally man and beast and the gods—the Canaanite woman recalls this: around the table there may be a little dog, a cat, a bird hoping for crumbs (Mt 15:27); and when Abraham sees the eternal Lord appearing to him in the form of three visitors in the shade of an oak tree and does not feel up to a conversation at their level, he offers them some cakes, some cheese, milk, a bit of veal— things that might be found in their mouths as well as in his (Gn 18:1-8). . . .

At table, the food gags the talkative and saves face for the silent. The beautiful young woman chews, the ugly woman becomes a guest, the engineer swallows with less gusto than the man with a mental disability, and certainly less avidly than the infant. Finally, the traitor can be served from the same dish as the saint (*Truly, I say to you: one of you eating with me now will betray me*, Mt 26:23). Look at them all, on an equal footing with regard to a meal, more so than with regard to death. And this is the truly Catholic religion. It does not demand that we adhere to an ideology or a jargon. It simply expects us to open our mouths wide together—and to know how to gulp: *I am the LORD your God, who brought you up out of the land of Egypt. Open your mouth wide, and I will fill it* (Ps 81:10).

He who eats my flesh and drinks my blood

You can give a coin to a tramp to buy a clear conscience from him (which incidentally teaches us that our conscience was in his possession). We might also sit down and chat with him to share our rather long-winded wisdom with him, or to lend him an ear, slightly deaf, but punctuated by understanding nods. The best thing, no doubt, is to share a sandwich and a glass of cheap red wine with him. Then we enter into truly common poetry. We eat from the same dish, at the same level, in keen proximity, and it is not unlikely that the tramp will teach us a thing or two about appetite.

We sense, however, that this is not enough. Conversation starts over the snack, but it quickly reaches its limits: the mouth that speaks makes itself less well understood than the full mouth. Therefore the full mouth should be at the same time the mouth that speaks. And the sandwich should also be the word of truth. And the cheap Cabernet should be the wine of the Kingdom. Or, conversely, the big philosophical question, "What is it?" should be as communicable and nourishing as good bread (that is where the name of manna comes from: *man ou?* in Hebrew, and in English: "What is it?").

The disciples on the road to Emmaus recognize the Risen Lord in the breaking of the bread, and at that very moment he disappears, and at that moment the disciples recognize themselves, too: *Did not our hearts burn within us while he talked to us on the road, while he opened to us the Scriptures?* (Lk 24:32). The most astonishing thing is not that they did not recognize Jesus when he walked with them, but rather that they had not recognized themselves with their hearts aflame. The interpretation of the Scriptures had not been enough—it was necessary for the Light to sit down at table with them, it was even necessary for It to become food so as not to just touch the intellect, but also to penetrate life down to its most rudimentary features: *I delight to do your will, O my God; your law is within my heart* (Ps 40:8). The Risen One evaporates into thin air, but he also becomes something solid: their daily bread. He had already been made flesh; now he becomes their table companion and refreshes their flesh. He is no longer there for them to look at but for them to feed on; he is no longer there for their instruction but for their construction.

This is the communion that Jesus institutes by his Holy Table, which is simultaneously far beneath and far beyond all doctrines (although there is nevertheless a dogma to express it).

P.S. For my pastor: From the preceding, Father, you could draw some hasty liturgical conclusions. For example, you might infer that the Eucharist ought to unfold unceremoniously as though chow were being served. That would be exactly the reverse. Instead you should conclude from it that the plainest chow should be experienced as an act of thanksgiving, and that our intestines should appear to us as a primordial and truly edifying rosary.

VI

IN ACCORDANCE WITH THE SCRIPTURES

And beginning with Moses and all the prophets, he interpreted to them in all the Scriptures the things concerning himself. . . . Then he said to them, "These are my words which I spoke to you, while I was still with you, that everything written about me in the law of Moses and the prophets and the psalms must be fulfilled." Then he opened their minds to understand the Scriptures.

Luke 24:27, 44-45

[The rich man suffering in the flames of Hades] said, "I beg you, father, to send Lazarus to my father's house, for I have five brothers, so that he may warn them, lest they also come into this place of torment." But Abraham said, "They have Moses and the prophets; let them hear them." And he said, "No, father Abraham; but if some one goes to them from the dead, they will repent." He said to him, "If they do not hear Moses and the prophets, neither will they be convinced if someone should rise from the dead."

Luke 16:27-31

If Christ has not been raised, then our preaching is in vain and your faith is in vain (1 Cor 15:14). This statement by Saint Paul is bizarre, to say the least. In principle, with a testament, the opposite happens: the message is fulfilled only inasmuch as its author is quite dead. And all literature, in this respect, is by nature a testament. It always develops starting with the author's absence. When he is not there to speak to us, then we are able to read his work. And only when he has entirely ceased to be of this world can his work be entirely incorporated into the world of literature.

Then nothing remains but his books, his style, his ideas, his characters, and one can assimilate them unreservedly, dedicate university professorships to them, have the sense that we are profoundly in league with the author, claim to feel better understood by "Hemingway" or "Melville" than by one's close friends, because "Hemingway" and "Melville" are names on a book cover and no longer those flesh-and-blood gentlemen who still live somewhere on earth and might deny our intimacy or our understanding with them.

If we are to believe his wife Catherine, whom he divorced after giving her ten children, Dickens would have appeared much less agreeable if we, like her, had lived with him. But now he is accessible only through his novels and thus can remain in our eyes the most cordial, the most charming man. Similarly, Socrates has been our dear friend ever since he drank the hemlock. Had he truly stood before us, we no doubt would have chimed in with his judges in condemning him. What literature proposes is therefore exactly the opposite of the Gospel message, if we are to believe Saint Paul.

A vain message and an illegible presence

Physical presence has its heaviness, its embarrassments, and even its odors. It sets up obstacles. French philosopher Michel Houellebecq remarks: "In a conversation one does not surrender as completely as one does in front of a blank page to an unknown addressee." From the reader's perspective this can be translated as: one is not as completely receptive in a conversation as in front of a page blackened by a known writer. Just let the poet and the wise man croak and, although they were cursed during their lifetime, they will be blessed after their death. Their message will be communicated infinitely better, and everyone will be able to interpret it in the sense most favorable to him. And then it is always more convenient to have a message *in* our hands rather than its messenger *on* our hands (imagine for a moment that it is not this little book but me sitting on your bedstand, and I think that we will rather quickly agree—you, me, and your spouse—that is a somewhat awkward situation).

With the Bible, however, it does not work in the same way as with the book. The message is in vain if the messenger is not alive, sitting on your bedstand, or at least waiting at your door (he is a decent fellow, after all). The message itself tells us: He is there, behind the wall of what is visible. *Behold, I stand at the door and knock; if anyone hears my voice and opens the door, I will come in to him and eat with him, and he with me* (Rv 3:20).

But the very fact that the message is so insistent in telling us that the messenger is here implies that the mere apparition of the Risen One is not enough. We need this insistant message. We need this apparition to be put into perspective by the Scriptures, which are our real eyeglasses. Saint Luke especially hammers this home in his post-Resurrection narratives. The two apparitions, the disciples on the road to Emmaus and then in the Upper Room, are arranged according to a meaningful symmetry: in the first, Jesus comments on the Bible, then sits down at table; in the second, he sits down at table then comments on the Bible. Several chapters earlier, in the parable of the rich man and poor Lazarus, he had attributed to Abraham this terrible saying: *If they do not hear Moses and the prophets, neither will they be convinced if someone should rise from the dead* (Lk 16:31). As though he were saying, in counterpoint to Saint Paul: "If the message is not heeded, the Resurrection is hollow."

If Jesus appeared just like that in the middle of your living room, but this apparition was not enclosed in the monstrance of the revealed Word starting with Moses, the prophets, and the Psalms, you would be incapable of grasping its significance. You would take him for Zeus, Mary Poppins, or a traveling salesman, not for the Messiah. Moreover, this is what I suppose: Jesus has already appeared repeatedly in your living room, between the ficus tree and the sofa-bed—unless it was in your dining room—but since you were not able to decipher his presence, he passed through unnoticed. You were unable to see him with your ears—or hear him with your eyes. If his message is in vain when we interpret it without him, his presence is illegible when we see it without the Scriptures.

The descendant's Ascension

A resurrection without the Bible is almost as sentimental and meaningless as a Christmas crèche without the genealogy of Christ. Then we get emotional about a little baby between Mary and Joseph: we celebrate the happy event of the nuclear family, with the ox and the ass on either side standing in for distant relatives, who will soon be replaced preferably by a poodle and Wi-Fi. In the latter case we admire the new man who has torn himself away from our earthly condition: it is the glory of the liberal individual who has escaped all by himself, like a big boy, like a self-made man or, to put it in less vague terms, like an Antichrist.

Then we shift almost imperceptibly from the Jesus of the Gospels to the character Bounderby in Dickens' *Hard*

Times: "A man with a pervading appearance on him of being inflated like a [hot-air] balloon, and ready to start [on its journey]. A man who could never sufficiently vaunt himself a self-made man." This rich entrepreneur conceals the existence of his mother to make people think that he was thrown as a baby into the gutter and owes his high social status solely to his own industry. If you call him a "son of a bitch," he is glad; he has attributed this title to himself for a long time, because it allows him to prove to you that he is above all the "son of his works." In spite of all that, is he not the heir of a (mother) tongue? No, he is an autonomous subject, a user of language, in agreement therein with the most modern philosophies, and storing in his wallet arguments that are valid in all languages. And so he believes in the resurrection, of course, as self-reconstruction and escape from history. And he weeps before the crèche where there is only the little child left on the straw, who will soon succeed, however, in getting out of the cow dung all by himself.

Nothing could flatter our pride more than this greeting-card Nativity: divine descent without being a human descendant. This is why Matthew begins with the genealogy of Jesus, from Abraham down to Joseph (Mt 1:1-18). And nothing could be sweeter to our vanity than a fantasy-film Resurrection: a heavenly ascension without earthly roots. This is why Luke traces his ancestry, from Joseph back to Adam, and therefore back to God, without any short-circuit, passing through seventy-seven generations (Lk 3:23-38). Now, the Evangelists are capable of tracing this genealogy back through time because the Risen Lord became a rabbi. He reread the Scriptures with his disciples. He showed them that his Resurrection was not coming to abolish but to fulfill the history of Israel.

The One who sums up and redeems history

It is actually more tremendous to be born of Jane and Robert than to issue from Jupiter's thigh. Take any character at all, situate him back in his family tree, and you will hear a song that comes from the depths of the ages. Dionysius poses no problem; he is outside of history, so transparent as to be nothing but an ancient god, which is to say a symbol. But what are we to say about Joe Schmo, the son of John Schmo and Betty, born Adjaho? He cannot be traced back to Mount Olympus, he is not the symbol of some universal force, he is not an archetype but an ordinary guy, and therefore someone more obscure and more transcendent.

For him to exist, ordinary as he may be, it required the unlikely intersection of two lines of ancestors, one of them going back initially to Ireland, the other to Africa; if we investigate further, however, they discreetly cross all the major historical periods, the World Wars, the Great Depression, the wars of Independence, the colonial era of the Kingdom of Dahomey, the Middle Ages, Rome, neolithic painted caves, Paradise lost, the creation of the universe. . . . All the species that followed one another in macroevolution, all the people who lived and died after having given life, and, finally, the T-Rex, Tautavel Man, a hominid subspecies, Joan of Arc, the Brazzaville Conference—all of that existed to lead today, however hard it may seem to conceive, to Joe Schmo.

His commonplace appearance is a detail in an epic vaster than *The Iliad*. His ordinary birth connects him, through the meanderings of love and chance, to a network more mysterious than the World Wide Web. Had he been a fallen angel or an earthbound god, his fabric would have been less noble, less precious: it would not have crisscrossed the woof and the warp and all those chains, an imbroglio of sons that would baffle even the Fates.

Joe Schmo is much more than a star—he is a son. A star reflects films, albums, sports achievements; a son reflects the origins of humanity, of which he is the current crowning glory. Yes, Joe Schmo, who is in charge of logistics at M&M's, is also the result and the guarantor of the whole history that preceded him: the fact that he should become a simple, decent man justifies in a certain way all the tortuous begettings that led to him: the alcoholic father, the grandmother who practiced witchcraft, his great-great-grandfather the bank clerk. *Each tree is known by its own fruit. For figs are not gathered from thorns, nor are grapes picked from a bramble bush* (Lk 6:44). This is true also of a family tree. Once a fig or a tasty bunch of grapes sprouts on it, the thorns and brambles of the past are over and no longer an obstacle. The tree is suddenly redeemed by this mature fruit. For the human fruit can, by grace and by its freedom, renew the sap and surpass the roots. This is its glory. But it is also its cross. It must carry that branch that bore it.

Every man, inasmuch as he is a son, is a candidate for messiahship—even Joe Schmo (and even his sister Joan). At this point my reader may feel that he has been swindled: "He told us that Jesus had already come into our living room or to our dinner table and that we had been unable to recognize him. But we see what he is doing. In fact, he did not mean to speak about Jesus, but about Joe Schmo or about some other bore of the same sort, highlighted by a review of history from the Big Bang down to him, so that, from this perspective, we should welcome as the Messiah any oddball precisely because he is neither a star nor a prelate, but merely because he is a son or a daughter!" To tell the truth, we already knew this at the end of our Magdalenian investigation into the body of the Risen One. It is now a question, rather, of remembering another law that allows us to see the meaning of the Incarnation and the Resurrection.

The fruit can redeem the tree, we said. It would be enough for a simple, decent man to be born in order for that to justify all of history. But where is that innocent man, awaited for centuries? Where is the man who is divine enough to be simple and decent? Better (or worse) than Antigone with her incestuous ancestry: here he appears in the line of David the adulterer, and also of the wicked kings Joram, Uzziah, Ahaz. . .all the way back to Adam, the first of all sinners. But God's grace is so abundant that even Joe Schmo, in charge of logistics at M&M's, once he becomes simple, can in turn become co-responsible for Salvation.

Letting the Bible read us

When the Risen Lord reads the Scriptures, he points out *the things concerning himself.* That goes without saying: he is not only the Savior announced in them, he is the Word of God. There is not a single verse that is not auto-biographical. Everything in the Bible is for him only an anecdote, and this is why he can interpret it *with authority* (Lk 4:32). For there is nothing anecdotal about a true anecdote. It presupposes a direct, living grasp of the event that is related, as in the stories that a traveler tells at a dinner, which stay in your memory for ever, more than any pages you may have read. Here again, the table remains the means of the highest form of communication.

The scribes and the critics are incapable of reading the Bible in this way, not because they do not read it enough, but because they read it too much. They analyze it in minute detail, read between the lines, fill in the gaps with archeological discoveries, publish works of their own on the question, hide the reality beneath their insightful volumes while ignoring Saint John's warning in his Gospel: *There are many other things which Jesus did; were every one of them to be written, I suppose that the world itself could not contain the books that would be written. . . . But these are written that you may believe that Jesus is the Christ, the Son of God, and that believing you may have life in his name* (21:25; 20:31).

It would be a mistake therefore to think that the Bible is an interpretation. It is not an interpretation. It is a key for understanding. It requires the reader to move from an interpretation of the text to a world that is legible, from a general wisdom to a story that concerns us personally, from writings about the life of Christ *to life in his name* (Jn 14:13).

Without this key for understanding, glory would be only a hypnotic spectacle, and the very name of God would become meaningless. We would be mistaken about what this name means. We would think that the worst possible thing would be "to make oneself out to be God," whereas one psalm declares: *You are gods, sons of the Most High, all of you* (Ps 82:6). The danger is not to make oneself out to be God, but to consider this name without the biblical key for understanding. For if we take this name according to the interpretation it gives, the real tragedy is instead that we do not make ourselves out sufficiently to be gods or messiahs, that is, sons of the Most High. If we were to strive to be like the God that the Scriptures speak to us about, we would be slow to anger and merciful, we would love every creature tenderly, we would be self-effacing so as to make room for it and to communicate to it the freedom to come to us or to rebel, and we would pardon it even when it went so far as to crucify us unjustly. . . . Nothing makes you humbler than to acknowledge that you are divine.

The Bible shows us how much we reject this divinization in favor of man-made idols, and consequently the extent to which we are dead and in need of resurrection. It turns the spotlight back on our heart, an experience about as flattering as expecting to see Prince Charming in the mirror and finding only a putrefying zombie. Scholars double down on the scientific character of their reading in order to avoid this unpleasant surprise (being read like a book when they thought that they were the ones doing the reading). They strive to be enlightening—so as not to be enlightened. They set themselves up as impartial judges—so as not to be judged. Finally, in order to avoid seeing the plank in their own eye, they become their brother's oculist.

VII

OUT OF BREATH: SAYING GOOD DAY AND FORGIVE ME

On the evening of that day, the first day after the Sabbath, the doors being shut where the disciples were, for fear of the Jews, Jesus came and stood among them and said to them, "Peace be with you." When he had said this, he showed them his hands and his side. Then the disciples were glad when they saw the Lord. Jesus said to them again, "Peace be with you. As the Father has sent me, even so I send you." And when he had said this, he breathed on them, and said to them, "Receive the Holy Spirit. If you forgive the sins of any, they are forgiven; if you retain the sins of any, they are retained."

John 20:19-23

The Resurrection of Christ is exactly the opposite of the reanimation of a corpse. It is even more unlike such a reanimation than death itself. It is not difficult to imagine the misfortune of a physician endowed with such a power: he revives a dead person, and now that dead person, once again as spry as a cricket—but unlike a cricket, having no instinct for how to move about in the world—immediately asks him this rather embarrassing question: "Very well, Doctor, but to what, to whom shall I dedicate my life now? You decided that I should do another tour of duty, and no doubt you have a good reason. . . . Before I was alive just like that, without any reason, because that was the movement of life, but now that you are *making* me live, you must have some explanation." The reviver is so taken aback by his revived patient's question that he advises him to go lie down for a while: he'll feel better after a good night's sleep. . . . But as soon as his great benefactor turns his back, and in the absence of any response on his part, the revived person has nothing more urgent to do than to hang himself. And of course, as soon as the physician discovers his patient dead a second time, he hurries to take him down off the rope and to re-reanimate him, only to lecture him: "Really, sir, you should not be so ungrateful for the benefits of science!"

"But then couldn't your science, which provides me with this extra longevity, tell me the meaning that goes with it? Forgive my stubbornness, a reanimated human is tougher than a mere mortal, but either there is a meaning, and it is worth giving my life for it, or else there is none, and then why shouldn't I kill myself?"

"But immortality. . .isn't immortality good?"

"You want to immortalize your stupidity, and I don't blame you, that's only normal; otherwise you'd be completely stupid. . . ."

It's not worth continuing. You have already guessed the punch line: unable to tolerate these pesky questions any longer, the physician euthanizes the man whom he had snatched from the jaws of death. This goes to show that the search for immortality and the practice of euthanasia are of the same ilk: in both cases it is about domination over life, but, since science and technology are called upon at the same time to provide the reason for this perpetuation—which they are incapable of doing, inasmuch as their methodology rules out all metaphysics as a matter of principle—we go immediately from the first to the second: we exterminate the reanimated.

In this little allegory, please note, the victim of the reanimation is still rather conciliatory. If I had to take a less accommodating subject, or let's say even the most unbearable and angriest of all reanimated humans, I would have looked for him among the saints. A saint would have additional reasons to resent the overly benevolent doctor. Not only would the latter have deprived him of his safe passage only to expose him once again to the peril of rejecting grace *in extremis* [on his deathbed], but furthermore he would have snatched him from the beatific vision. This is why only a God can afford to risk the reanimation of a corpse. Jesus raises up the widow's son, the daughter of Jairus (while commanding that they give her something to eat right away), or his friend Lazarus, but the reason why he indulges in this indiscretion of going and calling back someone from the clutches of death is because he simultaneously gives him the possibility of dying finally for something that is truly worth the trouble. If our physician had revived a saint, the latter would not have been content to condemn this thoughtlessness; he would have exhorted the physician to martyrdom as well.

This is the essential point. Not immortality, but martyrdom. Not the reanimation of the dead, but the reawakening of the living. If there is no simple joy in living, there can be no happiness in returning to life, only the stubbornness of a *ghost*. And there could be no joy in living unless there is someone to whom to give one's life (for life is fruitfulness). And so the presence of the Risen One is not in the first place the instrument of some external reanimation, but rather the sacrament of an interior resurrection that is already at work now: a renewal of one's breath, a transfiguration of vital fluids that coincides with the most supernatural power, which is also the most necessary for everyday life (I am still speaking to you, darling)—the power to give and to forgive, the power, not to preserve one's own petty life (the principle of bourgeois ontology), but to welcome life in a way that is abundant enough to give it.

Against devotional dualism

When Jesus appears in the midst of his disciples—without walking through the wall, please recall, but arriving despite the locked doors, as a clandestine passerby, which implies that he was already there—his first words are: *Peace be with you.*

Right away, the very spiritual commentator will mention the descent of peace from heaven like a featherless dove and will deploy such stratospherically magnificent images that they will go right over your head, because as he speaks you happen to have a bad cold and are annoyed by bureaucratic complications, worried about the uncertain outcome of the football game between the Patriots and the Seahawks, anxious about new threats of terrorist attacks. . . . And there you are, afflicted by the same schizophrenia so widespread among believers: rosy clouds in the sky, shifting sands on earth. . .and Yours Truly bobbing up and down between them like a yoyo.

Now Jesus wants to keep us from precisely this dualism. His first words, heard in their context, do not separate heaven and earth but on the contrary bring about their unity. *Peace be with you,* in Hebrew, is *Shalom aleikhem,* namely, the most common, the most ordinary words of greeting. To our ever greater astonishment, the Messiah came, he was put on the cross, he descended into hell, he rose again on the third day, and you might expect that all this supreme adventure would be to bring back for us from the depths of the abyss some pearl of wisdom that would be impossible to throw to the swine; but no, it is to pronounce a word that even the swinish use regularly: "Hello."

The cure: saying "Good day" and meaning it

I have often thought of writing the story of a man who no longer dares to speak for fear of lying. His fear is not of grandiose, imprudent theoretical formulations. It concerns everyday words. If someone calls, he deems it presumptuous to answer: "I'm here"; he knows all too well that he is never entirely present. If someone asks him his name, he thinks it deceitful to state his identity in the terms recorded in his official papers; he knows all too well that these syllables do not completely express his person. Not bothered by such scruples, the competent authorities do not hesitate to throw him in jail; all the more so since, when they asked him whether he was guilty of murdering Mrs. Smith, his neighbor in the apartment down the hall, he found it too much to give an unqualified yes or no. (He remembers times when he did not look at her and help her with all the charity he could have.)

Philosophers will no doubt describe him as a skeptic. In reality, he is a man amazed by language. He is dazzled by the absolute that each word promises. When the sun shines or the ravioli has been cooked well, he is prompted to declare: "The weather is fine," or "The ravioli is excellent," but a sort of modesty restrains him. The sun also shines upon misfortune here below, so it's not really that fine. And these squares of dough filled with spinach do not really meet the the highest standards of excellence—for he's not even sure the spinach was labeled "Fair Trade," and therefore they cannot be called altogether excellent.

One day he begins to feel toward a young woman some of those sentiments that cause you to panic even more than usual. How can he tell her: "I love you"? This is his deep desire and at the same time it would be a bold-faced lie. Besides, he does not even dare to say "Good day" to her, because in order for those words to be true, the day would have to be absolutely good, goodness would finally have to spread throughout the world. . . . He is not a Christian, but one day, one of those days that is not absolutely good, by chance or out of boredom he enters a church, arrives toward the end of a Mass and hears this prayer that the faithful say while striking their breast just before receiving Communion: "Lord, I am not worthy that you should enter under my roof, but only say the word and my soul shall be healed." This is what he had always sensed: it would take just one word, someone would have to say just one thing, but say it in truth, in order for immense healing to extend to all souls.

So supernatural and so routine

How can anyone say "Good day"? Evil has been done. It is impossible to act as though it had never happened. Hence it can bear down with all its weight—the weight of remorse in the offender, the weight of rancor in the offended party—so much so that the daylight becomes burdened with a black, suffocating smoke. How can you change something that is irreversible? What can be done to change dead weight into a surge of life? It would take a supernatural intervention: God alone is capable in all justice of resetting the counters to zero or, to put it a little more accurately, of *overturning the moneychangers' tables* (see Jn 2:15). But this supernatural intervention is required by the most ordinary life: each of us can only really get up in the morning as though to a new *day* by transcending all the piled-up grievances, all the accumulated bitterness, all the stored-up hatreds, not only against others but especially against oneself. Without forgiveness, there is a future, but there are no prospects: a person buys but no longer redeems, the cancer develops its metastasis, the machine carries out its program without any encounter or respite.

In order to say "good day" truly, therefore, nothing less than a salute is required, combining in itself the most familiar and the most supernatural of things: for the root of the word "salute" is "salvation." There has to be that second wind that is more original than the first. There has to be that Spirit who brings unity in differences and

116

in disagreements. There has to be his power of forgiveness which is stronger than fate and even stronger than fatigue.

The Risen One says *Shalom* and breathes on his Apostles. This is a clear reference to the creation of man, when the Eternal *breathed into [Adam's] nostrils the breath of life* (Gn 2:7). This is because it is about a new creation here. And the fact that this new creation is connected with the power to forgive sins makes it as simple and surprising as the future. A power that reassures, certainly, but is all the more terrible because of it.

For this power warns us that we will sin again. On the one hand, nothing is ever lost, everything can be forgiven; on the other hand, nothing is ever permanently achieved, one can become a backslider and even refuse forgiveness—which is worse than backsliding, since it is wanting one's sin to be *retained* (Jn 20:23). Life in the Spirit makes us hope against all hope but also very wary of all sense of security. It opens up prospects but does not guarantee the future. It is a divine life. It is also a simply human life, but one in which "good day" is not just an empty expression.

The more truth there is, the more need of forgiveness

A certain experience in my family made me understand that forgiveness was less necessary to be reconciled with enemies than to live with close relatives. First of all, a

117

grand reconciliation with a major enemy flatters our ego. The pride that we derive from it can lead us to it, more than mercy. Whereas with reconciliation in the family, there is nothing to boast about: it is unceremonious mercy, a chivalrous deed without the horse and armor. Being a hero requires less heroism than being a husband or a father. The hero is inspired by greatness to confront a furious giant; the father experiences the humiliation of being disarmed by his daughter's outbursts of temper. And when the hero succeeds in smoking the peace pipe with the giant, he makes the front page in the newspaper; but what renown does the father get from the fact that his daughter finally speaks to him politely at breakfast?

Then too, only the ones we love can bring us close to committing the perfect crime. They do not need to have any special cunning or malice. It is just that they live with us, in our space, know how to get under our defenses, know every chink in our armor. And there they are, attacking right at the moment when you are about to go to sleep, or when you are not even fully awake. It's not that they were lying in wait; it's just that familiarity makes us neglect the appearances we would normally keep up in society. In the hallway, the kitchen, the bathroom, all it takes is someone at the end of their tether to cross paths with someone feeling a little vulnerable. . . . We squabble in the family more often and with fewer scruples than among political adversaries. And since the love we have for one another makes us deeply vulnerable, the blows can pierce our heart directly without touching the flesh, without even making the slightest scratch.

Finally, if you are a Christian, it only makes things tougher. With barbarians, we resign ourselves. With strangers, we are careful. With "brothers"—and Peter's question to Jesus is in fact: *Lord, when my brother sins against me, how many times shall I forgive him?* (cf. Mt 18:21)—we say things to their face, we blame each other for not being saints, and thereby risk despairing of ever becoming so ourselves.

The more truth there is, the less comfort; and it becomes necessary to forgive each other seventy times seven times more. Christ warns us that, in his light, family relations will be doomed to divisions that the darkness had preserved them from: *Do not think that I have come to bring peace on earth; I have not come to bring peace, but a sword. For I have come to set a man against his father, and a daughter against her mother, and a daughter-in-law against her mother-in-law; and a man's foes will be those of his own household* (Mt 10:34-36). How can people go on in the midst of these daily frictions without forgiving each other more and more?

If I make some affectionate gesture toward her, my dear and tender wife can't keep from getting everything off her chest. In order to become completely receptive to my affection, she has to dump out on me all the

119

grievances weighing on her soul. This is a legitimate way of proceeding, and a sign of great confidence. For her it is a matter of accepting my bouquet of flowers by pouring out onto my head a whole cartload of trash—my own trash, I admit—and for me it is a matter of continuing to hold out those flowers even though they are no longer that fresh and my desire to offer them is completely gone. At that moment, I suddenly daydream about being hailed by an unknown, charming damsel who asks me to free her from the clutches of cruel but easily influenced bandits. I have to admit though, the most chivalrous spirit is not found in this cliché of the knight in shining armor. It is found in the sequel to the story, about which the fairy tales are very evasive—when, all this time after the prince has married the princess and they have had many children, the unknown, charming damsel begins to resemble the cruel bandit. . . .

In short, the woman of my life has to become the death of me before she can become the woman of my resurrection. I therefore have to forgive this woman who torments me by asking me to ask her for forgiveness. To communicate with her not just through our façades but also through our cellars, our pits, our dungeons. The occasion for it may seem petty. Nevertheless our faithfulness in these little trials is what enables us to withstand the big ones.

VIII
PLACE YOUR
HAND
IN MY SIDE

Now Thomas, one of the Twelve, called the Twin,
was not with them when Jesus came. So the other dis-
ciples told him, "We have seen the Lord." But he said
to them, "Unless I see in his hands the print of the
nails, and place my finger in the mark of the nails,
and place my hand in his side, I will not believe."
Eight days later, his disciples were again in the house,
and Thomas was with them. The doors were shut, but
Jesus came and stood among them, and said, "Peace
be with you." Then he said to Thomas, "Put your fin-
ger here, and see my hands, and put out your hand,
and place it in my side; do not be faithless, but be-
lieving." Thomas answered him, "My Lord and my
God!" Jesus said to him, "You have believed because
you have seen me. Blessed are those who have not seen
and yet believe."

John 20:24-29

In the episode on the preceding page, Jesus breathes: not on the twelve Apostles, but on ten of them, because Judas hanged himself and Thomas is absent. Ten is the number of the just whom Abraham bargained for in order to call off the destruction of Sodom (Gn 18:32). It is also the number of servants that Gideon enlists to pull down the altar of Baal (Jgs 6:27). Finally, there are the commandments on the two tablets, and the fingers on two hands. And nevertheless, despite the transparency of the symbolism and the warm vote of confidence for the decimal system, it will be necessary to go back to twelve. The quorum is non-negotiable. So Luke reports the replacement of Judas by Matthias, before Pentecost can take place (Acts 1:15-26). And John recounts the return of Thomas, just after the gift of the Spirit has taken place. In his Book of Revelation, the heavenly Jerusalem will be founded not on one, nor on ten, nor on eleven, but on these twelve, who reflect the twelve tribes descended from the twelve sons of Jacob. This is a pledge that the Church continues the line of Israel and that she is one only in multiplicity. She is neither a house of one ethnic group nor an incubator of clones, but an improbable collection of motley people, who bear the marks of the most unlikely histories.

I am like Saint Thomas. . .

So Thomas missed the call to the first apparition in the Upper Room. He spoiled everything. He did not receive the Holy Spirit (which, all told, is even more annoying than walking right past your own life or marrying a mutt instead of your fiancée). And what is worse (or because of that), he does not want to believe what his colleagues tell him, even though their number far exceeds what the law requires for valid testimony.

That would be enough to rank him among the unluckiest and most stubborn. But he tries for the gold medal for arrogance to boot. Indeed, he sets such an extreme condition that even the most arrogant of individuals would not make when parroting the stupid saying: "I am like Saint Thomas: I won't believe it unless I see it." For, if they really were like Thomas, they would have to have the terrible audacity to declare: "I won't believe it unless I put my finger into it. . . ." Which, in the case of believing in the existence of a door, could do them considerable harm, and, in the case of believing in the presence of their boss, would put them in an awkward situation that could cost them their job.

And it is not just anywhere that Thomas wants to probe his finger or even stuff his whole paw. It is in the holes made by the nails, into the gash made by the lance. . . . Along with the prize for arrogance, no doubt he intends to win the crown for being morbid. Here, the proverbial saying becomes downright unbearable since, strictly speaking, it would have to be formulated from now on: "Me, you know, I am like Saint Thomas. I only believe in that which I can probe the wound."

A hothead

But first, why this absence of the one they call *Didymus* (in other words, "Twin")? Skipping out in that way doesn't just make him a bad student. It associates him with the traitor who committed suicide: he inevitably looks like a brother, a double of Judas. Everyone knows why *he* is not here. Because he killed himself. But why isn't Thomas here? Is it not precisely because he wants to be killed. . .?

To verify this, we need only return to his two other interventions in the Gospel according to Saint John. The first is when Christ decides to travel toward Jerusalem to see his deceased friend Lazarus. There, Jesus clearly faces death threats, he and his disciples, too, because of their obvious complicity. So his companions say everything they can to draw him up short: why take such risks for a corpse? And even if you plan to revive him, you don't rob Peter to pay Paul—or, rather: you don't revive Lazarus only to get killed yourself. But then, just when everyone else is balking, Thomas exclaims: *Let us also go, that we may die with him* (Jn 11:16). Our Apostle is therefore a go-getter and a hothead. He is in the starting blocks, in pole position to follow Jesus anywhere or even nowhere.

His big question during the Last Supper corroborates this hypothesis: *Lord*, he asks, *we do not know where you are going; how can we know the way?* To which Jesus replies: *I am the Way, and the Truth, and the Life* (Jn 14:5-6). Since Thomas was the first to whom these words were addressed, we can imagine his despair after Golgotha: the Life is dead, the Truth has fallen silent, the Way has wandered off among the shades. Off we go, then, once again to follow him! Let us follow in the footsteps of the one who is now the Dead End, the Silence, and the Death!

And so, while the ten Galileans barricade themselves behind *the doors [that were] shut. . .for fear of the Jews*, he is strolling around outside, his neck in plain view, his chest an easy target. He is not afraid, not he: the crucifixion is the last word of the Word, so let's listen to it! He begs the centurions, the scribes, all the doctors of the law that he runs into; maybe he will even go call on Herod and then the high priests and then Pilate, begging that they grant him this favor: "Could you please pound nails through my hands and feet? I am a disciple of the man whom you just put to death as a usurper and a blasphemer, so would you kindly do me the favor of preparing a gibbet like his on top of Mount Calvary. . . . I would even settle for a little decapitation, you know. . . . Or a thrust of the lance here, which could pierce me to the heart. . . . I would even go so far as to temper my ambitions and let myself be hanged with a piece of cord from this tree right in front of us, although that might damage my reputation and make me appear more a renegade than a believer. . . . How about stoning? Wouldn't a nice little collective stoning have the twofold advantage of satisfying me and providing you with a way to let off steam and do some male bonding?"

But there is no limit to human wickedness. Cruelly, relentlessly, those whom he hopes to turn into executioners kindly reply: "Calm down, my friend. Your grieving will pass. Have confidence in yourself! Regain your zest for life! Look on the bright side! You just have to 'work through' your grief. Admit it, you were deceived. We've opened a crisis counseling center for you. This is called Stockholm syndrome. . .or maybe a case of Diogenes syndrome. . .unless it is Münchhausen's syndrome. . .or maybe a Peter Pan complex. . . ."

Eternal wounds

In such circumstances, when his fellow disciples tell him that they have *seen the Lord*, that takes the cake! He asks nothing better than to die like his master, and this honor is denied him a second time. The executioners were so inhumane as to try to cheer him up, and now the Apostles inform him of something that utterly ruins his plan: his master is alive. In order to follow him, it is no longer a matter of just being killed, he has to be revived as well—which even the most competent, compassionate executioner could not offer you. We can understand why Thomas is distraught. The reason why he is unbelieving is because he believes in a cross without glory.

But there is yet another side to his unbelief: faithfulness itself, which corresponds to the rejection of glory if it is not with the cross. Thomas knew the depth of despair:

he saw the Way lead to the abyss, the Life swallowed up by the tomb, the Truth engulfed by a lie, and now all of that was just playacting? Jesus in the coffin was nothing but a jack-in-the-box? The murderous injustice was only a mirage? No, all that must have been quite real. The thrust of the lance cannot be wiped away with a sponge. Its victim cannot be reduced to a hero in a musical comedy who sings in the midst of his sufferings, "Baby, baby, why did you leave me?" and during the finale finds himself with the Baby in question in his arms, humming "What a wonderful world. . ." as though nothing at all had happened. If that were the case, what about our responsibility? What would be the coherence of the story? The happy ending shouldn't give the impression there had been no tragedy. The dawn, however beautiful it may be, could not forget the horror that preceded it—and may yet follow it. If it were to forget, it would no longer rise on the horizon: it would descend like an artificial light trained on us by an extraterrestrial spaceship.

Thomas senses that glory, in order to be true, can only be the reverse of a simple miracle. In a simple miracle, the wounds disappear. In glory, they must remain gaping wide. If they were no longer there, quite visible, very deep, then glory would be nothing but an optical illusion, a pain killer, a diversion. And yet, at the same time, with these holes that make our sins for ever clear to see, how could that still be glory? We would have to break down with remorse rather than jump for joy. We would have to scourge ourselves for it rather than take pride in it. How then can the truth of glory be compatible with the no less essential truth of the cross? Thomas has no idea. But where Johann Sebastian Bach sings *Jesu, joy of man's desiring*, he shouts all the louder: "Jesu, gaping wounds still bearing, grant that I may die of shame."

If we denied a single fact about this world

Things are so tightly interwoven that if we try to unpick one little thread, everything unravels. Deny a single fact about this world and you end up denying the entire world. This denial is nevertheless a rather common practice. Indeed, it is one of humanity's favorite pastimes. Sherlock Holmes may admire the mysterious disappearance of the Orient Express, its locomotive along with eighteen cars. But anyone at all can make the universe disappear for you just like that, in the blink of an eye.

As soon as work is over, quick, you put yourself into a lotus position, regulate your breathing, squint toward a point midway between your eyes and arrive at such a state of interior tranquility that, no, it's definitely not possible that that venomous Aunt Agatha who causes you so much trouble really exists! Or else you undertake scientific research simply because you cannot look at yourself in the mirror: you look for the hidden structure of reality, descend to the nanometer, at a scale where a living thing is no longer distinguishable from a non-living thing, where parts crumble into particles, where injustices give way to equations. . . .

Thomas rejects these escape routes. He is such a spoilsport even the harmless enjoyment of a picnic would appear to him criminal blindness. He would be astonished you could so nonchalantly down your food; he would immediately bring up all the children dying of hunger at that very moment on the other side of the world— and you would feel so guilty you would start thinking of sending them your leftover cold cuts and potato chips by Overnight Express. He wants the Risen One to sit down at the picnic with his wounds, and us not to be afraid to stick our fingers into them as though into the back of our throat, and then see whether our joy is strong enough to overcome the urge to vomit.

He who doubted in good faith

And he will get his wish. Jesus appears once again, says, *Peace be with you*, in other words, "Good day," presents his wide-open wounds to him, and orders him to go right ahead, without any embarrassment: *Put your finger here, and see my hands, and put out your hand, and place it in my side; do not be faithless, but believing.*

This granting of his wish disconcerts the Apostle to the point of flipping him over like a pancake. The one who tends to the most radical doubt suddenly makes a profession of faith more exalted than any other that you can find in the four Gospels. Others indeed had called Jesus "Messiah" or "Son of God"; he bluntly calls him "my God." Doesn't this display a tendency to exaggerate after having been so reticent?

His profession of faith, obviously, testifies that what he believes does not coincide with what he sees. For what he sees is a resuscitated man, a creature therefore, however radiant he may be; and what he suddenly believes is that this creature is also his Creator. No, really, he goes too far. After irritating us in one way, he exasperates us in the other. After pitting the cross against glory, he recognizes the Almighty in the Crucified. A moment ago he had been ruining your appetite by talking to you about children dying of hunger, and now he ruins your disgust by finding God under a wound. Frankly, I can't see who would want to have him for a guest either at a wedding banquet or at a funeral reception. He had already been such a pain of a spoilsport, and now he is completely unbearable with his ill-timed beatitude.

We know his Lord's response: *You have believed because you have seen me. Blessed are those who have not seen and yet believe.* The second statement could very well refer to the Evangelist who reports these words: he is the one who believed without seeing, or having seen only the rolled-up napkin and the shroud spread out flat. Is John trying to show off? Or is it the opposite? What if this remark means that it is easier to believe without seeing—without seeing what Thomas saw, without touching what he touched?

If the friend whom you betrayed came back and shoved right under your nose the wound that you gave him by stabbing him on the evening of his birthday, if he invited you moreover to plunge your hand matter-of-factly into his pierced heart and told you that he suffered all that for you, you can bet that, even if you were blessed with the greatest composure, you would soon feel your legs irresistibly itching to run away. Thomas stays. And we notice that this bad Apostle resembles the good thief. Sunk in despair, he missed the Holy Spirit and made every effort to have someone string him up on the gallows, and yet here he is suddenly more confident than the others, so much so that, according to tradition, of all the first missionaries, he was the one who went the farthest (running off after all, not in flight, but rushing right toward Christ there), to Persia, perhaps to China, in any case to southern India where he founded seven churches between Kerala and Sri Lanka, before finally enjoying the good fortune of having his throat slit by a "high priest" near Mylapore for having melted down a metallic idol by the mere breath of his prayer.

What does this teach us? That we must not approach the Truth while playacting the role of a believer. That we must not pretend to adhere to the faith of the Ten. The problem is not doubt but half-measures. If you doubt, do so thoroughly, and may your doubt be in good faith (indeed, it would be unfortunate to doubt and to believe too much in yourself). Argue that the existence of the Kingdom seems to you incompatible with the existence of Aunt Agatha; most importantly, object that it is incompatible with your own abjection when you order two scoops of Chocolate Macadamia Nut at Ben & Jerry's while someone has just spoken to you about children dying of hunger. Be Cartesian about it, go even farther and ask the following question: what makes such a doubt possible? Why do we not have the unquestioning placidity of cattle? Why are we so scandalized by evil? And what can we do to keep this scandal from making us its accomplices? Well, then, let us admit it: if we doubt (and there's no doubt about our doubt), it is because our hearts, in spite of ourselves and in spite of everything, demand the Truth: we would not have this thirst for Truth in us if the cheap wine of our petty opinions was enough to satisfy us. And if the cross seems to us absurd to the point of driving us to renounce joy, the reason is because we hope for an even broader joy capable of taking up and transfiguring all the wounds of history.

IX
BACK
TO FISHING

Jesus manifested himself again to the disciples by the Sea of Tiberias; and he revealed himself in this way. Simon Peter, Thomas called the Twin, Nathanael of Cana in Galilee, the sons of Zebedee, and two others of his disciples were together. Simon Peter said to them, "I am going fishing." They said to him, "We will go with you." They went out and got into the boat; but that night they caught nothing. Just as day was breaking, Jesus stood on the beach; yet the disciples did not know that it was Jesus. Jesus said to them, "Children, have you any fish?" They answered him, "No." He said to them, "Cast the net on the right side of the boat, and you will find some." So they cast it, and now they were not able to haul it in, for the quantity of fish. That disciple whom Jesus loved said to Peter, "It is the Lord!" When Simon Peter heard that it was the Lord, he put on his clothes, for he was stripped for work, and sprang into the sea. But the other disciples came in the boat, dragging the net full of fish, for they were not far from the land, but about a hundred yards off.

John 21:1-8

Suddenly everything seems as pleasant as a cold shower and as effective as a sword stabbing the water. The Risen One appeared to the disciples; he sent them as he himself was sent, and, instead of hurrying away then to proclaim the Good News to the four corners of the earth, they behave as if nothing had happened, as though everything had been only a dream; back to square one!

If we compare the Gospel of John to the Gospel of Luke (5:1-11), the loop is even more striking. In Luke, on the same lake, there is the miraculous catch of fish that precedes the call of the first disciples, and therefore the very beginning of their adventure. Then they *left everything* to follow Christ. And here they are, starting all over again!

A comparison of these two fishing expeditions, the one before the Passion and the one after the Resurrection, seems (all things considered) to mark a regression rather than progress. In the first, Jesus was in the boat; in the second, he is standing on the shore. For this reason, back then, he could speak the exciting words, *Put out into the deep*; now, because he is within earshot, they must be close by the shore, *about a hundred yards off.* Then the nets were full to breaking point, so that it took two boats almost sinking under the weight to bring them ashore; now one net is still full, but one boat is enough to bring it in, and the Greek text even ends by referring to it as only a "little boat. . . ."

In order to avoid this impression of dullness and backsliding, this scene is usually isolated and subjected to a symbolic interpretation: their vain efforts during the night and the following dawn are the Death and the Resurrection; the right side where the net is cast is the pierced side of Christ from which gush the Church and her sacraments; the one hundred fifty-three large fish that are caught correspond to the number of peoples in the known world at that time, and therefore catholicity; stark naked Peter who puts on clothing to jump into the water is redeemed Adam who receives baptism, etc. These are all gold nuggets that deserve to be sculpted on the capitals of a Romanesque basilica, but they don't manage to answer the basic question posed when the episode is put back in the sequence of events with which it does not appear consistent, unless it is to recall the fable of the mountain that gave birth to a mouse: the encounter with the living God which ought to make you like the angels ultimately leads you back to being a fish seller.

Nevertheless I have my own idea about the subject, and, in order to confirm it, I asked some historical-critical exegetes whether they didn't think this passage had been written and added later—that is, according to my calculations, around the year 2000, after the digital revolution had swept through all of society. If this is the case, its meaning would be crystal clear: to recall, in the age of the network, what a net actually does.

And the Word was made carpenter

The Risen Lord had told them almost two weeks earlier: *As the Father has sent me, even so I send you.* Just how did the Father send him? Brandishing lightning bolts direct from the sky? By having him deliver sermons from his mother's breast? No, rather by making him a carpenter. For this reason every good Christian family should aspire to have a son in carpentry, and if he cannot reach that godly position (since the jobs are rare and training expensive), let him become a shepherd at least, or a vinedresser, or a fisherman, or if need be a tentmaker like Saint Paul. . . . Of course I am not unaware of the fact that some parents steer their children toward degrees in business or engineering, but no doubt they do so out of humility because, after all, somebody has to give up having a real job in order to do the dirty work of evangelizing the dregs of Wall Street or of M.I.T.

Though a notable fact, in times past, people did not dwell on this too much: the Word took on flesh not in order firstly to be a priest or a preacher, but in order to work with his hands; and not to work with any old material, but with the material par excellence, wood, a living thing that calls on us to extend its leafy growth; and in order to make with this wood not sculptures or matches, but houses, and maybe boats—let's just say arks of all kinds. Nowadays this fact seems remarkable to us, because we no longer know how to make very much with our own ten fingers. This is

136

the great moral catastrophe of our era. Gaston Bachelard suggested that Jean-Paul Sartre went astray, not primarily in his ideas, but in his hands: "No doubt it would have been a humane act to put Roquentin, the hero of the novel *Nausea*, in front of a big block of wood to be smoothed and planed. That would be enough to happily teach him that oak doesn't rot, that wood repays dynamism with dynamism, in short, that the health of our minds lies in our hands."

With the development of virtual reality, we tend to think that everything can be reduced to elements—bits, atoms, neurons, genes. . .BANG!—exploding natural forms so that they seem malleable according to the whim of the moment. . . . Thanks to this stupefying scheme of things, someone who does not know how to change a bicycle tire and would not lift a finger to help an elderly neighbor carry her shopping thinks that he is capable of bending the universe with the touch of a finger (and he justifies himself by saying that the old lady who has difficulty walking only had to surf to have her shopping delivered to her door). He plays *Civilization VI*. And he loses sight of—or touch with—the consistency of reality. He becomes credulous to the point of supposing that Google is more important in life than a field of turnips. (I like turnips a lot, which quite obviously does not rule out praise of peas, nor an apologia for the meadow where goats graze, nor, *a fortiori*, a panegyric to the fish-filled sea.)

Starting from this observation, the relevance of our Gospel passage jumps out at us. It seems to have been written yesterday, or tomorrow, whatever the specialists may say. For, in the age of the Apostles, this loss of presence to the world was rarer: then they had the Jordan Valley, not Silicon Valley. Today, the spade, the fishnet, the shepherd's crook, or the plane seem more than ever to be a prerequisite for the apostolate. The meaning of the Incarnation involves the meaning of the flesh, since openness to the supernatural does not distort nature but rather returns us to its source. Anyone who has not experienced the order of things with his own hands can only pay lip service in preaching the One who orders these things. He is not realistic enough to bear witness to the Resurrection.

Media man and medieval man

Everyone is ready to denounce the obscurantism of the Middle Ages, but that is only to console ourselves for the false dawn of our own media age. Medieval man was much more positive than the multimedia citizen. He built his house, sewed his clothes, tilled the soil, buried a number of his children in it, frequently ran across lepers, danced with the whole village around the big bonfire on Saint John's eve, removed his hat before a statue of the Blessed Virgin, killed the pig, and armed himself with a scythe or a pitchfork to welcome the tax collector. A rough-hewn fellow whom you didn't mess with.

Maybe he was wrong to think that the earth was flat, but he was much closer to it, clearing the ground, hoeing it, breaking it up, sowing it; whereas our view of a round, blue planet adopts the imaginary perspective of an astronaut floating in the middle of nowhere, for whom the wheat does not sprout or mature but appears directly in plastic-wrapped extra-soft slices. And maybe he erred in thinking that the sun revolved around this terrestrial pancake, but it was the bright measure of his days, longer in the summer, shorter in the winter; and he also knew the benefits of rain, whereas, for us tourists, rain is only bad weather, and our days, reduced to timetables, are ticked off on a Taylor digital timer.

And so, necessarily, the event of Someone rising from the dead seems difficult to swallow for someone who is used to avatars, online profiles, and 3-D objects that are neither born nor dead nor alive. But for a positive fellow of yore who was good with his hands, a peasant, a miller, a tanner, it was unlikely, no doubt, and yet no sooner did he hear: *Truly, truly, I say to you, unless a grain of wheat falls into the earth and dies, it remains alone; but if it dies, it bears much fruit* (Jn 12:24), than it became a simple matter; it was as true as April, the renewal of the greenery, the gold of the harvest. . . .

Father vinedresser

The lesson goes beyond the one that we already received concerning the meal of the Risen One (we live on good—fish—soup, not only on fine words). It proposes that we acknowledge this subtler truth: techniques close to creation make one much more disposed to accept redemption than a hyper-sophisticated technology. Why do I say "techniques" and not "thoughts"? Because our mentalities, ultimately, are influenced less by concepts than by gestures, tools, the production methods all around us (the reader will excuse me for being a bit Marxist here). The manner in which we see things depends less on our point of view than on how we use our hands (as the etymology of the word "manner" suggests, from the Latin *manuaria*, "concerning the hand").

The "Greek miracle," the advent of philosophy as a preparation for accepting the Good News, is often put forward. But long before that there was the "Late Stone Age miracle." If I ever bumped into the guy who invented the hoe and enabled his brethren to transition from gathering to farming, I swear to you that I would hug him as cordially as Aristotle and Plato combined, or even more so. We do not appreciate the upheaval that this brought about in the intellectual order. Most of the images used by Christ and the Bible to depict the life of the theological virtues are drawn from the field of agriculture. That is also where we get our words "cult" and "culture" (so much so that it must be said, without wishing to upset anyone, that incense is more closely related to manure than to air freshener, and that a great poem resembles an orchard or plowing claggy soil more than a novel by Danielle Steel).

During his last meal before his Passion, Jesus tells his disciples: *I am the true vine, and my Father is the vinedresser* (Jn 15:1). When Saint Paul explains the mission of an apostle, he tells the Corinthians: *I planted, Apollos watered, but God gave the growth* (1 Cor 3:6). Agriculture serves as an analogy for the divine Work—more than craftsmanship, and unlike engineering. The model of engineering is mechanical: the model of agriculture resembles the Socratic method. The engineer imposes forms on nature understood as a stockpile of energies and materials; the farmer accompanies the deployment of a natural form of which he is not the maker. The first can increase the speed of production, he is master of the cadence; the second knows that you can't make grass grow by pulling on it, and he is wedded to the rhythm and the circumstances of the seasons.

If our thinking is more imbued with engineering than agriculture—and this has been the case at least since the second half of the twentieth century—then our *manner* of thinking about the spiritual and apostolic life is turned completely upside down as a result. God no longer has the patience of the vinedresser. He has the meddlesome fiddlyness of a mechanic. And his votaries will follow this

141

example. Everything will be viewed in terms of our push-button society. It will be thought abnormal that a sermon is not immediately effective. People will demand obedience as responsive as a light switch. We will ask for forgiveness, but soon accuse the offended party of not changing his attitude toward us, as though his complicated feelings had to turn around as fast as a webpage downloads.

The new arch-apostle soon sinks into fundamentalism, not because he is archaic, but because he is high-tech. He wants others to react to his harangue as quickly as an Intel processor. And he forgets that, according to Jesus, the average spiritual reactivity that a preacher has a right to hope for from his listeners is much inferior than that of a tortoise or a snail. Instead it is that of a plant: the sure slowness of sprouting and taking root. He said so explicitly: *Where the seeds had not much soil, immediately they sprang up* (cf. Mt 13:5).

Fishers of sinners

But then why fishing, in this case, and not field work? Why this Early Stone Age activity that can immediately haul in piles of fish where one has not sown? Because it is precisely a matter of sowing and not of growth—of calling and not of raising. The agriculture model is concerned rather with sanctification; the fishing model, rather with proclamation. The first has to do mainly with the listeners who receive the word; the second, with the disciples who proclaim it. The latter are *fishers of men* (Mt 4:19). But, once caught, their big fish become sheep and shoots, and they must become shepherds and vinedressers.

What does this fishing model entail for the proclamation of the Good News?

First, whereas the hunter follows trails along which there is a shelter every so often, the fisherman leaves *terra firma* to venture out onto the uncertain, moving waves, with no refuge or path: the storm is his portion and drowning his probable destiny.

Second, the hunter can see, tail and track down his prey, and decide on the moment when he hits him with his arrow. The fisherman generally acts blindly. He casts his line and waits for something to bite. Often he toils the whole night in vain. But even in daylight, his success is entrusted to the darkness beneath the sea.

Third, if he fishes with a net, he uses neither hook nor harpoon: he does not choose his prey. He traps them in living groups, without distinction, even though the breadth of the mesh may generously allow the ones that are not the right size to swim through.

This then is the art of minimal control and maximum trust. Even more than in agriculture, one relies on the randomness of the weather and gathers the fruits of a fecundity that is not ours—the fecundity of the sea, which is at the same time a threat of death without burial and a dark cradle of life.

We should add that, although one *takes up* weapons, in contrast one *lets down* a net. Catching with a net is done by first letting go. And this is why the one who makes the catch is always surprised: his catch could be anything. There, in his parish, sailing under the flag of goodness and beauty, there he is with sharks, shrimps, bottom feeders, guppies. There are even crabs, eels, sardines, rays, codfish, monkfish—in short, everything astonishing that under-sea fauna has to offer. Although it takes all kinds to make a world, it takes even more to make the Kingdom.

X

PAPAL INDIGNITY

When they had finished breakfast, Jesus said to Simon Peter, "Simon, son of John, do you love me more than these?" He said to him, "Yes, Lord; you know that I love you." He said to him, "Feed my lambs." A second time he said to him, "Simon, son of John, do you love me?" He said to him, "Yes, Lord; you know that I love you." He said to him, "Tend my sheep." He said to him the third time, "Simon, son of John, do you love me?" Peter was grieved because he said to him the third time, "Do you love me?" And he said to him, "Lord, you know everything; you know that I love you." Jesus said to him, "Feed my sheep. Truly, truly, I say to you, when you were young, you fastened your own belt and walked where you would; but when you are old, you will stretch out your hands, and another will fasten your belt for you and carry you where you do not wish to go." (This he said to show by what death he was to glorify God.) And after this he said to him, "Follow me." Peter turned and saw following them the disciple whom Jesus loved, who had lain close to his breast at the supper and had said, "Lord, who is it that is going to betray you?" When Peter saw him, he said to Jesus, "Lord, what about this man?" Jesus said to him, "If it is my will that he remain until I come, what is that to you? Follow me!"

John 21:15-22

There is something much better than winning the lottery: falling seriously ill then experiencing recovery. I owe this remark to a man who had just emerged from the long paralysis of locked-in syndrome: "It's more extraordinary than winning the mega-jackpot!" he exclaimed. Now what was so extraordinary in his opinion? The most ordinary things, obviously: being able to stretch out his hand, stroke the face of his daughter, get up out of bed, put one foot in front of the other. . . .

This impression is not just the psychological effect of relief. It corresponds to an ontological truth. After all, the mega-jackpot comes from the national lottery, whereas our existence comes from God, which is after all much more impressive. We suggested this in the introduction: the superhero has superpowers, but these superpowers rely on ordinary powers without which he would be nothing: breathing, the senses of touch, sight, hearing, taste. . . . We marvel that Spiderman climbs walls, but at the origin of our amazement is the mason who built the wall and our perception of it through our senses. These essential phenomena are nevertheless so well concealed beneath ingratitude and banality that it is necessary to be deprived of them in order to appreciate the gift.

And this brings us neatly enough to what we could call the primacy of Peter. Why is he the first pope? Because he was made capable of assessing things at their true value. And why was he made capable of this? Because he had been the biggest zero. He had descended to the depths of his nothingness, and so he can appreciate the least little twig as an unprecedented grace.

Triple trouble

A pontiff is a bridge builder. Now a bridge is necessary only to pass over an abyss. The Supreme Pontiff therefore can only be someone who has experienced the supreme abyss. Prince of the fall: that is how the Gospels, unfazed, present Simon Peter to us. A clown act, you might say. Every time he exalts himself to the heights, there he goes and falls flat on his face in the depths. Moreover, everything begins in his case with a double-edged miracle: Christ hits him with the cure of his mother-in-law (Lk 4:38-39). This gives fair warning that Peter's task will not be for the faint of heart. After this incident, there will be no end to his roller coaster ride.

When he asks Jesus to command him to come to him walking on the water, he takes a few steps on the surface and then unfortunately starts to sink (Mt 14:28-30). When he declares that Jesus is *the Christ, the Son of the living God*, Jesus replies that this profession of faith comes not so much from his lips as from his Father who is in heaven (Mt 16:17). When, at the first prediction of the Passion, he exclaims as a considerate friend, *God forbid, Lord!* Jesus calls him *Satan* (Mt 16:22-23), a term that he will not even use to designate Judas. When he is present at the Transfiguration and proposes to set up three tents for Jesus, Moses, and Elijah, a cloud descends from the sky to make a mockery of his camping plans (Mt 17:4-5). On the night of the Last Supper, when he swears his unshakable faithfulness—*Even though they all fall away, I will not*— even though he hears Truth in person tell him *this very night, before the cock crows twice, you will deny me three times,* our enthusiast, proud of having finally accepted the idea of the Passion, insists that even *if I must die with you, I will not deny you* (Mk 14:27-31). We all know the dismaying sequel: he does in fact deny him, three times, and not in the presence of threatening soldiers, but before a poor old servant. Such a career is enough to make you want to hide your head and wonder where poor Peter found the courage not to slit his own throat just to keep his cheeks from blushing bright red with embarrassment.

To tell the truth, we know the answer. What gave him courage, what raised him up from his death of shame and turned his admitted nothingness into a vessel of faith was Jesus' special prayer for him: *Simon, Simon, behold, Satan demanded to have you, that he might sift you like wheat, but I have prayed for you that your faith may not fail; and when you have turned again, strengthen your brethren* (Lk 22:31-32). And this is indeed what happens, contrary to all expectations. The one who had failed to walk on the water, plunges into the lake. He casts himself after having cast the net, and then, according to the remark by Saint Augustine, he makes "a threefold profession that compensates for his threefold denial."

Here again, however, a sort of problem remains. Jesus asks him two times, *Do you love me?* using the Greek verb *agapaô*, which refers to divine charity. Peter stubbornly replies with the verb *phileô*, which refers to human friendship. Is he going astray once again? Is he so thick-headed that even his Easter finale is one last train-wreck?

I think, rather, that he no longer presumes on his own strength. From now on, he does not claim to love *more than these*. He trusts his own judgment less than the Lord's (*you know that I love you*). Most importantly, though he aspires to it, he does not claim a supernatural love which is beyond him (hence his pained expression, the third time, when Jesus scales down his question to more modest proportions by asking him this time whether he loves him, with the verb *phileô*).

Peter's humility brings him to a final reversal. The Risen Lord tells him, *Follow me*, and there he goes, immediately: instead of following him, he turns away from him. An odd sort of obedience. Strict obedience, nevertheless. For, although he turns away, it is only to turn toward *the disciple whom Jesus loved*. The one who wanted to be the best now cares only about his brothers. *Lord, what about this man?* He remains convinced he is less important, less worthy than the others. And this is precisely what makes him worthy to be the vicar of Christ.

The joy of feeling unworthy

What has this got to do with the paralytic about whom we spoke before? My wife says that the decisive teaching in this passage is that the incarnate Word is not afraid to ask *the* question of sentimental girls: "Do you love me?"—although Peter tends to answer him only in the loutish manner of a male like me: "Look, you know very well; don't you remember what I promised you on our wedding day?" This interpretation is interesting. She says that this passage is about recognizing here one final abasement of the risen Christ, almost baser than the cross—to the level of starry-eyed sentimentality—and about learning to say unceasingly and still passionately "I love you" to my wife—which is considerable progress on behalf of the "civilization of love." Yet, with all due respect, my darling, I would like to attempt a different commentary here (which, however, is not unconnected with yours).

What can be done so as not to be blasé? What is the method for rediscovering the world (and therefore our wife also) each morning with the gratitude and amazement of someone who suddenly emerges from total paralysis and even from total deafness, total blindness, from a complete loss of taste and smell, etc.? Peter shows us the method, and it is infallible. It consists of always feeling unworthy—which is easy enough if one is honest with oneself. Chesterton sees this feeling of unworthiness as the golden key, and even as one of the keys of Saint Peter:

"The only way to enjoy even a weed is to feel unworthy even of a weed."

The problem is that instead of cultivating this feeling of unworthiness that disposes us to be grateful for the smallest things, we drape ourselves in worthiness in regard to the best things, which never seem good enough for us. We claim instead a whole litany of rights—"the right to happiness" that causes us to lose the simple joy of living, "the right to a child" that prevents us from welcoming a child as it comes, "the right to freedom of expression" which kills our wonder at the fact of saying "Good day.". . . I have nothing against these rights, of course, but if you focus primarily on them, it is obviously the quickest way to sink into bitterness and recriminations: "We say, like the bad-tempered Major in the club, 'Is this a chop fit for a gentleman?'" This attitude can only lead to "the actual loss of all appetite for the chop or a cup of dandelion tea."

In reality, this feeling of unworthiness is in harmony with our highest worthiness, which is a concave worthiness, the worthiness of a creature and a redeemed one at that, the worthiness of a vessel and a channel of graces. Teresa of Ávila found no better way to celebrate God's beauty than to exclaim: "You expand our nothingness." The more one recognizes that one is empty, the better disposed one is to receive. The more one receives, the more one's capacity increases; in other words, one's power as a jug, which can only make us still humbler—recall that a jug, which in French is commonly used as a metaphor for the starry-eyed sentimentality mentioned above, is also an image that the saints are fond of using for themselves: they perceive themselves as little jugs beneath the waterfall, benefiting from the water only to slake the thirst of others.

The happiness of accusing oneself

This feeling of unworthiness results from an ontological truth and not from a psychological contortion, as we already said. The fact is that we did not make ourselves, and our creation is an utterly unmerited gift. To live as a creature would be enough to make us permanently receptive and full of gratitude, if it weren't for pride. Therefore there has to be something else that pride cannot tolerate. And this something else is to acknowledge that one is a sinner.

Of course, even this can be faked. Pride does not always wrap itself in sovereign, haughty dignity. It can also make the feeling of unworthiness withdraw into itself and turn it into the rejection of what is offered. But to think that our misery precludes our receiving any mercy is also to set ourselves up as the final judge and therefore to fail to understand the extent to which we were miserable. At the very beginning of his relationship with Jesus, right after the first miraculous catch of fish, Simon Peter implores him: *Depart from me, for I am a sinful man, O Lord* (Lk 5:8)—a feeling of unworthiness that still smacks of pride, because despite everything I am the one who decides whether or not I am worthy, and I remain at the level of retribution, shirking the order of grace. At the end, after his three denials, Peter considers himself still less worthy, but his pride is destroyed, and now he can beg with genuine humility: "Come close to me, for I am a sinful man."

There is nothing like beating your breast and admitting your guilt to make you marvel at everything, even at a big slap in the face. Dorotheus of Gaza takes this as the principle for ever-joyful hospitality: "The cause of all our troubles is the fact that we do not accuse ourselves. In reality, even if we had done a thousand good deeds, if we do not accuse ourselves, we will never stop suffering and causing others to suffer, thus wasting all our efforts. On the contrary, when someone accuses himself, what joy, what rest he would bring with him wherever he goes!" Indeed, if someone thinks that he deserves to be whipped because of his sins, then the most resounding slap will appear to be incredible clemency. And if you think that you are fit to be strangled at the hands of an executioner, the mere fact of continuing to breathe proves to be an extraordinary privilege.

But the best thing, no doubt, is to consider oneself deserving of hell—and even that would require a very great grace from God. Then all calamities seem to you to be a reduced sentence. Seeing that instead of the infernal

punishments that you deserve, you merely get some earthly suffering, one that you can still offer to the Almighty—
such as no longer being able to *fasten your own belt* or
being crucified head-down—there is still something in
that to be thankful for.

Being a (Holy) Father

A headhunter, even a Christian one, will not fail to object:
the first pope was recruited on the basis of previous experience any personnel officer who was the least bit conscientious would find prohibitive. *The stone which the builders
rejected has become the cornerstone* (Ps 117:22)—right! *He
lifts the needy from the dung heap* (1 Sm 2:8)—not to worry!
But with such principles I doubt that you would be a success as a manager of human resources.

This is all very true. It is appropriate to point out,
nevertheless, that the Church is a family, not a business,
and that the pope is a father, not an expert. Now everyone knows that human fatherhood is always accompanied
by a feeling of unworthiness and incompetence—for if a
man were to feel entirely worthy and competent to raise
a child, then he would be a terrible pedagogue, and that
child would be an orphan. . . .

Fatherhood descends on us like lightning. It is not
granted to us because we have earned a certificate of pa-
rental aptitude. It falls to our lot suddenly because we
slept with a woman—which in no way prepares us for the

art of changing a diaper or educating a child. There we are, suddenly with a baby in our arms and, no doubt, to stop his screams, we will learn little by little to stop trying to put him away in a drawer. We will strive, by the nature of things, to gain some qualifications, but that in no way changes our basic unworthiness, and the feeling of that unworthiness is precisely the most precious thing that we have to hand down to our sons and daughters.

First, it gives us the opportunity to show them that none of us is *the* Father, and obliges us to ensure they turn with us toward the eternal Father, *from whom all father-hood in heaven and on earth is named* (cf. Eph 3:15). This is the first educational mission, and the best professional educator, exactly because he claims to be without flaw or sonship, can only fail at it.

Second, insofar as we assume an authority founded on the mere fact of being the author (in this case, the be-getter) and not on any sort of competence, this feeling of unworthiness gives us the opportunity to communicate to our children confidence in life rather than the con-trol of production. The planner who already had a pain-less and all-drawn-up program for his descendant would quite logically, as the opposite of Gepetto, already have transformed him into a wooden puppet.

Third, in feeling unworthy to have a kid, we hardened rascals, who have nothing greater to hand on than our nothingness, will be able to consider even a little pest as a blessing. The smug man who would proclaim his right to have an heir worthy of his commercial enterprise could only change his little angel into a demon that would take revenge for having been treated like a trademark. A true father would never indulge in such arrogance. He is similar to the first Holy Father. His admitted inanity makes him capable of transmitting a truth greater than his own.

XI
TO ALL
CREATION

And he said to them, "Go into all the world and preach the gospel to the whole creation. He who believes and is baptized will be saved; but he who does not believe will be condemned. And these signs will accompany those who believe: in my name they will cast out demons; they will speak in new tongues; they will pick up serpents, and if they drink any deadly thing, it will not hurt them; they will lay their hands on the sick, and they will recover."

Mark 16:15-18

Are we going to start a dialogue with the dandelion and the slug? Is this the sign that differentiates the Good News from the latest news? (The victory of the Bulls over the Knicks is proclaimed exclusively to men and more specifically to basketball fans; Christ's victory over death also concerns mollusks, among other creatures, and must therefore be proclaimed to them clearly and appropriately.) The Risen Lord's command is categorical: *Go into all the world and preach the gospel to the whole creation. . . .*

The second imperative has repercussions on the first. It alerts us to the fact that *all the world* must be understood here not only in terms of extension but also, and in the first place, in terms of comprehensiveness. It is not enough to go to Borneo to evangelize the Malaysian Muslims. It is important also—and considerably more exotic—to stay in your neighborhood and to catechize Snookums, the chihuahua belonging to your neighbor, Mrs. Smith.

After all, Francis of Assisi preached a sermon to the birds and converted the ferocious wolf of Gubbio. As for our Lord himself, we see him addressing a fig tree, then encouraging his disciples to have a faith capable of commanding mountains to be cast into the sea.

Moreover, I take as examples here only natural beings, whereas *all the world* and *the whole creation* designate artificial products as well, and, à propos, it is rather obvious that your mobile phone needs a good talking to. At the risk of disappointing overly strict ecologists, who have a love of animals only and not of objects, it is necessary to proclaim the Gospel also to the casserole, the chandelier, the underwear, the dishwasher (so that it does not deprive you entirely of the satisfaction of scouring a pan and entering into genuine collaboration with this friend who rinses and this other friend who dries), and the television (so that it will pay close attention to what you say and will not interrupt your conversations with those near and dear to you at inopportune moments). I recommend to the missionary that he start by proclaiming the Good News to a wall—or maybe even to a loaded pistol aimed at his forehead. That is an excellent preparation for his encounter with his fellow human beings.

Some will think I am joking. I have never been so serious. It is of decisive importance not to reduce the Resurrection to a human-to-human event but to consider it in its cosmic scope. On the one hand, this prevents us from turning it into a petty consolation prize, a security blanket for grown-ups, a "spiritual option" or a "religious fact" that would not involve the whole material world, from the Higgs boson to the President of the United States, any more than a radioactive explosion would. On the other hand, this forces us to distinguish evangelization from propaganda: it is a question of bearing witness to something that is just as essential for a clam as for a star, for an alley cat as for the Oscar-winning actress Sandra

Bullock; it becomes apparent that the indispensable pre-requisite for proclaiming the Good News does not lie in communications skills or persuasive methods, because neither the star nor the clam nor even Sandra Bullock, to tell the truth, will really be receptive to them.

If it is a creature. . .

A Charismatic friend, who is accustomed to door-to-door visiting and street preaching, pointed out to me the ad-vantages to be gained by considering one's neighbor as a creature and not specifically as a human being: "When you tell yourself that the guy in front of you is a human being, and most importantly, a human being called to holiness, you run the risk of being terribly disappoint-ed and rushing right away into the realm of morality to reprimand him, point out his failings, and tell him that his swinish life is very far from his angelic calling. But if you tell yourself that this someone is a creature, just like a pig or a worm, then you are obliged to recognize that, for a worm or a pig, he is nevertheless a fantastic pig or an absolutely fabulous earthworm. For my part, if the gentle-man is aggressive, I classify him in the species of 'howler monkeys,' and at the end of the day I conclude that he is a rather nice one. If he is afflicted with senile dementia, I put him in the category of plants, and I must admit that, for a vegetable, he is the most awesome vegetable I have ever seen!. . . Esmeralda [in Hugo's *Hunchback of Notre Dame*] is afraid to look up at Quasimodo while she gladly pets his nanny-goat with its horns and hooves, so that Quasimodo groans, 'My misfortune is that I still resemble a man too much. I would like to be entirely a beast, like this she-goat.' If the Bohemian beauty had taken Quasimodo as an entirely separate species and not as a deformed specimen of humanity, no doubt she would have learned to cuddle up to him without disgust, just like a cute little lamb, which, if she were to judge it by classical ideals for the young male human figure, would appear to her like a hideous monster."

Rediscovering the wonder of the zoo to combat the disenchantment of aestheticism or moralism, seeing in one's neighbor a sufficiently indeterminate creature so that one still firstly thinks him worthy to exist—this seems to me to be a judicious method (even though it may lead, if applied literally, to regrettable confusions; for instance, putting the aggressive guy into a cage or making soup with the senile fellow). In any case, it agrees with certain fundamental assertions of theology. To see a being as a creature before anything else is to become certain that this being exists by the express will of the Creator.

This truth may be painful to admit, but it is irrefutable: if the Creator did not love this idiot, this idiot would not exist. Consequently, proclaiming the Gospel to a human being as a creature before proclaiming it to him as a human being compels us to say yes to his presence before preaching anything at all to him. Before "trying to do him some good" (which has always been the motto of all controlling people—from tyrannical mothers to total-itarian systems), we must acknowledge that it is already good that he exists: as stupid as he may seem to us, he is the will of Eternal Wisdom; as ugly as he may appear to us, he is a creation of Subsistent Beauty; then too, how-ever wicked he may be, he is in the first place the work of Almighty Goodness. Admittedly, this does put us into a tragicomical situation: the atheist who denies the word of God is himself a word of God (in what he is, not in what he says); and the fundamentalist who brandishes a destructive God is himself the concern of a God who is patient enough to put up with such a nasty little squirt.

In him all things hold together

The preceding discussion, you will tell me, returns to the human-to-human question that we claimed to have set aside. Where then is your fine bureaucratic project for in-ter-species dialogue, the evangelization of the weasel and the cactus, the ecumenism of the pebble—for if men re-main silent, *the stones will cry out* (cf. Lk 19:40), right? We have already conducted part of this investigation on the body of the Risen Lord. We met with it again in the bread and in our neighbor—both of them in the conviviality of the holy table. But we can go still farther and say with Saint Paul that from now on *in him all things hold together*

(Col 1:17). His prosaic apparitions are to teach us to be divinely simple. These are ways of accommodating the weakness of our eyes. As the collapse of the intact shroud insinuates, the glorious body in itself transcends the parameters of our space-time continuum. It is no longer so much that he is in the world as that the world is in him.

The poetry of love has always sensed this reversal of the situation—and here it is indeed a reversal of *situation* par excellence: the inversion of container and content, of landscape and figure, of human body and space. The beloved embraces the universe. The poet André Breton recites the litany thereof: "My wife with her wood-fire hair. . . My wife with eyebrows like the edge of a swallow's nest. . . My wife with champagne shoulders and of a fountain with heads of dolphins under the ice. . . My wife with her bosom of golden Valley. . . My wife with her back like a bird in vertical flight. . . ." This surrealism reconnects with the realism of love. The poet may well think that his technique is unprecedented, but it resembles the ancient poetry of the Song of Songs. The bridegroom says to the bride: *Your hair is like a flock of goats, moving down the slopes of Gilead. Your teeth are like a flock of shorn ewes that have come up from the washing. . .* " (Song 4:1-2). And the bride says about the bridegroom: *His eyes are like doves beside springs of water, bathed in milk, fitly set. His cheeks are like beds of spices, yielding fragrance* (Song 5:12-13). An interplay of metaphors, no doubt, but also, since the

Resurrection and the Ascension (and the Assumption too, for what applies to the woman), a metaphysical fact.

You want to encounter Jesus? You think that that is the rarest, most difficult thing in the world. Not at all. Encounter anything, quite plainly and simply. Encounter a drop of water. Encounter a peony. Encounter a pigeon. Encounter even a MacBook or a pimply nephew. If you really encounter them, in other words, feeling a certain giddiness when confronted with their mystery, then Jesus is there, who bears them up and even bears their sins and seeks to deliver them from them. Giving this name to the experience presupposes of course that one has learned to read reality in the Scriptures and to taste it in the Eucharist, and this already means: to *speak in new tongues* (to exclaim "Lord!" in the presence of a pigeon), to *pick up serpents, and drink any deadly thing* without being harmed (to use a MacBook without losing the meaning of presence), to *cure the sick and drive out demons* (to be assured that the Savior surrounds your pimply nephew with his tenderness and that the kid is therefore capable, contrary to all expectations, of leaving his Playstation and being receptive to the poetry of the Song of Songs).

Turns and detours of Providence

Previously, the creature was perceived in the love of the Creator. Presently, it is welcomed in the salvation of the Redeemer. The proclamation of the Good News thus overflows by far the framework of morality. Certainly there is nothing wrong with preaching virtue. But it must be conceded that vice can render many services. My friend Douve told me yesterday what had happened to her at the time of a miscarriage: as a result of a severe and dangerous hemorrhage, she had lost consciousness in the middle of the night while on the toilet, and it was her sister Cosima who saved her from a likely death by calling the emergency responders—because she had just come back from the nightclub. She alone was available at the hour when decent people were sleeping. Praised be the nightclub? That remains to be proved: the woman who was able to rescue her swooning sister at three in the morning would no doubt have been unable to hear her cries at noon. This combination of circumstances recalls, however, some stories from the Bible in which the contrast is even starker.

Joseph was sold by his brothers and consequently went through all the vicissitudes that led him to become Pharaoh's steward and, one day, to save his family from famine. (Thomas More writes in the margin of his Liturgy of the Hours: "To think that my worst enemies are my best friends, because Joseph's brothers could not have done him as much good by their love and favor as they did him by their malice and hatred.") Similarly, Rahab, being a prostitute, and thus having a house open to any late-night passerby along the walls of Jericho, can welcome and protect the Israelites and become one of the women named in the genealogy of Jesus—like the adulteress Bathsheba. All these immoral marvels, nevertheless, are no more than minor escapades compared with the cross of Christ, which saves the world by means of the most unjust torment. Does this mean that we should encourage torture, prostitution, or human trafficking with a view to the common good? That would be to submit to the prevailing moralism—the morality of a liberalism that exhorts us to strive to be egotists because, thanks to the invisible hand of the Market, private vices will make for public prosperity.

Anyone who proclaims the Gospel wants the Good, but his Gospel reminds him that this Good comes about according to *unsearchable judgments and inscrutable ways* (cf. Rom 11:33) that far exceed his legal injunctions and plans for evangelization. Providence is with him: *In everything God works for good with those who love him* (Rom 8:28). He has all of creation as his ally: *For the creation waits with eager longing for the revealing of the sons of God* (Rom 8:19). This does not mean that he does not have to act, nor that he should pursue his own interest and let come what may, as, in a parody of the theology of Providence, market theories would have us believe. On the contrary, his action must be open enough in order to have the power to assist at the birth of the universe. What he reveals, the birthing that he assists (for a wise man is always in a certain way a midwife) is not something superimposed on reality, but is the work of reality itself.

He should not exalt himself too much, however. It is a fearsome thing to have all of creation on your side. You are not crushed, perhaps, but you are *afflicted in every way*; you are not *destroyed* but still *struck down* (2 Cor 4:8-9). What happens takes priority over what you had planned. You must consider the most insufferable bore who rings your doorbell to be an envoy from heaven. Take comfort, though, in the thought that it is just as tough for him as it is for you. For you will lead him to recognize his surprising provenance; you will make the atheist feel that he is a word of God, and the fundamentalist that he is a sign of God's patience. Douve hinted to her sister that the Almighty was the one who had providentially sent her to the nightclub so that she could return at the exact hour—an exact hour that did not depend on her punctuality—when she would need her help: in the same way he had once thrown Jonah into the gullet of the whale so that the whale could spew him up on the shores of Nineveh. (Cosima no longer goes to the nightclub now, but she does sing in bars: old romantic songs that are in a way the profane replica of the Song of Songs.)

All the world and the kingdom of those near and dear

If *all the world* is all creatures, that is already a lot to do to evangelize it all, and often the most difficult in this field is not the ferocious bulldog but one's own family:

A prophet is not without honor except in his own country and in his own house (Mt 13:57). And all the more so as each member of the family can claim this title of despised prophet. . . . If you mention family, moreover, you mean in-laws too, and in-laws can be a clan with stranger, more ferocious customs than any lost tribe. We must agree, ultimately, that of all the creatures that rebelled against the word of God, our own heart is no doubt the worst, and that it has recesses wilder than the Amazon jungle. This is proof that life is well designed. You don't have to look far to find your circus or your courtroom. And since the earth is round, the remotest end of the world is right here.

Some, nevertheless, will hear the call to travel to the ends of the earth, sometimes to encounter societies less resistant than their own relatives: *Go into all the world*, in the extended sense—which does not mean "send text messages everywhere in the world." The Catholic missionary has nothing to do with the globalization of data. It is a matter of going there oneself, in person. Love of neighbor is never communicated better than by getting close. And the best way to evoke the mystery of the Incarnation is still to make yourself present in flesh and blood. When the disciples go out two by two, they preach that *the Kingdom is at hand* (Mt 10:7)—in other words, the Kingdom is experienced in proximity, and it is propagated from one individual to another near and dear to him: *repentance and forgiveness of sins should be preached in his name to all nations,* of course, but *beginning from Jerusalem* (Lk 24:47).

Above all, because *in him all things hold together,* to preach his Resurrection is to hasten to meet him over there where he already is, but without the natives realizing it yet. *He is going before you to Galilee* (Mk 16:7), and therefore also to Paris, to China, the foothills of Machu Picchu, or to the suburbs of Des Moines, Iowa. The missionary does not bring a foreign idol to these places. He reveals to them the name and the gift of something extremely intimate. His legs speed him on his way only to manifest deeper roots. And so he is not afraid to water this foreign soil with the blood that he received from his fathers.

XII
LAYING ONE'S HEAD ON THE CHOPPING BLOCK
(OR HANDING OVER ONE'S BODY TO BE STONED)

He, full of the Holy Spirit, gazed into heaven and saw the glory of God, and Jesus standing at the right hand of God; and he said, "Behold, I see the heavens opened, and the Son of man standing at the right hand of God." But they cried out with a loud voice and stopped their ears and rushed together upon him. Then they cast him out of the city and stoned him; and the witnesses laid down their garments at the feet of a young man named Saul. And as they were stoning Stephen, he prayed, "Lord Jesus, receive my spirit." And he knelt down and cried with a loud voice, "Lord, do not hold this sin against them." And when he said this, he fell asleep.

Acts 7:55-60

It is rather remarkable that most of those who saw the Risen Lord themselves died a violent death, thrown from the top of a temple, beheaded, stoned, disemboweled, crucified upside-down, flayed alive. . . . You don't have to be superstitious to discern in this something more fatal than the curse of King Tut. Except that in this case, as the victims themselves see it, we are not talking about a curse but a blessing: it resembles not so much Pharaoh's revenge as a new exodus from Egypt.

This disposition to martyrdom must not be mistaken either for a suicidal tendency or for capricious stubbornness. A suicidal tendency results rather from the search for comfort: someone absolutely wants to feel calm, and if we can no longer obtain the ease of the sofa, then there's always the rest of the coffin. Capricious stubbornness results, on the other hand, from the search for consensus: someone absolutely wants the other guy to agree with him, and if verbal persuasion fails, you can always fascinate him with blood. This resembles the blackmail of little children who threaten to hold their breath until you give them back their toy. The pseudo-martyrs are hardly any more mature. They claim to prove to you the truth of what they assert by splitting their heads open at your feet, which is really a lack of good manners (it doesn't bother them that they are spattering your nice clean slacks) and especially of fair play (they shut your mouth as effectively as someone who seizes you by the throat). How, after that, with their blood forming a big pool on your carpet, can you invite them to continue the conversation over a glass of wine?

Unlike such crude behavior, the disposition to martyrdom results from more basic good manners. First of all, it is not a death impulse but a zest for life—to the point of desiring eternal life. Next, it corresponds to the "After you" that we spoke about in regard to the Easter middle-distance running event and the empty tomb. The witness to the Risen One always lets his neighbor go ahead of him. Nevertheless, because he lets Christ go ahead first, and because in order to do that he knows the difference between a promenade and a precipice, his "After you" frequently takes the form of a *Vade retro* [Go back], without, however, changing in nature. The same politeness that makes you hold the door open so that someone else can go inside ahead of you urges you to block his path when the door in question is the gate of hell.

The tragedy is that the precipice often has the look of a promenade—the road to hell is paved with good intentions—and the path to paradise is the way of the cross. The person who is obliged to you mistakes you for an aggressor. He prefers his dark thoughts to hope, because at least his dark thoughts belong to him and fit in his head. He prefers his contentment to bliss, because at least his contentment keeps him safe from any heartbreak. Therefore he unhesitatingly thanks you by crucifying you, and furthermore you can't complain too much, since there is an odd clairvoyance to his misunderstanding. (The path to paradise leads by way of the cross—isn't that true for you too?) This is the adventure of Stephen, the first martyr and, since he is a spiritual majordomo or deacon officially appointed to *serve tables* (Acts 6:2-3), a great connoisseur of savoir-vivre.

Stephen, Saul, and Ananias

Christ appears again after the Ascension and Pentecost. This looks like a violation of the rule stated earlier, namely, that the purpose of the Resurrection is our life in the Spirit, and that the Mystical Body of the Risen Lord is now to be discovered in its members, in other words, in our neighbor. In reality, it is the exception that confirms the rule and, above all, affirms God's freedom.

The Acts of the Apostles records for us three of these extra apparitions—the first to Stephen, the second to Saul, the third to Ananias. All three appearances are distinguished from those before the Ascension by four features: First, they are private: only one person sees it while those around him see nothing—which was not the case on the road to Emmaus or in the Upper Room. Next, they are heavenly: Jesus no longer shows himself with the discreet familiarity of the man who walks and eats with his friends and reinterprets the Scriptures for them—he bursts in suddenly through a split in the heavens, at the right hand of the Father. Third, by way of compensating, they are immediately connected with martyrdom, as though a more immediate glory also implied more immediately the cross, or the moment of the vision coincided with the moment of the mission. Finally, this time to compensate for their private nature, these apparitions relate to enemies: what is at stake is no longer the faith of the women or of the Apostles, but rather the encounter between the persecutor and the persecuted, which is impossible at the merely horizontal level.

Stephen is so enthralled by what he sees that it spills over in his voice. Those who hear him are plainly more put off by it than opera buffs by a bellowing tenor: they stop their ears and throw at him, not tomatoes, but big stones that his blood will take care of reddening. Among those who stone him, as their head and cloakroom attendant, stands Paul. He is the one who will be the beneficiary of the second apparition, the result of the prayer of Stephen, whose last words under the hail of stones repeat the first word of Christ on the cross: *Lord, do not hold this sin against them.*

Soon afterward, Saul was thrown to the ground on the road to Damascus, where he was traveling to round up and kill others *belonging to the Way* (Acts 9:2)—I recommend that fashionable circles readopt this old name. If you say right away: "I am Christian," people will think you are ridiculous; but declare: "I belong to the Way," and they will think that you are remarkable (and maybe even a Freemason). Now, while he is dazzling Saul on the road, Jesus appears at the same time in Damascus to one of the people Saul was preparing to throw into prison. Ananias too is floored: he learns that the *enemy of the saints* has become *a chosen instrument. . .to carry the Name* of the Savior (cf. Acts 9:15), and that he must go and look for him *on Straight Street, in the house of Judas* to baptize him and restore his sight. . . .

The last three apparitions in the New Testament are intertwined so that those who were starting to collide might enter into communion. The persecuted, the persecutor, and the one who was about to be persecuted by the latter and therefore spoke ill of him: these three adversaries meet one another on high and come together here below. For such an event to happen, it was not enough to "lay the stones of a constructive dialogue." Or rather, it was, but Stephen first had to take these stones of expectation and dialogue full in the face.

Proposing a toast

I spoke earlier about conversing cordially over a glass of wine, and it is appropriate to strive as much as possible to do so in a candid, friendly manner. But here's the thing: good manners teach us not to lift the cup to our lips without having proposed a toast. And that is where the pleasant atmosphere can tank, matters can be spoiled, and the cup—however delicious the liquor that it contains may be—can turn bitter. To what, to whom shall we propose a toast? To good health? To life? Most times we stop at words that are left intentionally vague so as not to give rise to conflict. Honesty demands, nevertheless, that you go somewhat deeper into the question: good health to do what? And what are the source and the destination of life?

Cardinal Newman, in his letter to the Duke of Norfolk, writes: "Certainly, if I am obliged to bring religion into after-dinner toasts (which indeed does not seem quite the thing), I shall drink—to the Pope, if you please,—still, to Conscience first, and to the Pope afterwards." Conscience appears to be a less controversial toast than the pope, but, when you actually reflect on it, it may be even more painful. After all, conscience is an organ that escapes our control just as much or even more than our shameful parts: it stiffens when we would like to be relaxed, it torments us when we would like to sleep, it warns us when we would like to have its approval. And this is why, ordinarily and out of prudishness, people prefer talk about sex to conversation about conscience.

In short, if we take our toast really to heart, here is what happens: "Cheers, Stephen!"—and then all the candor and camaraderie blow up, because it is supposed to turn into friendship in the truth. The first martyr only tried to offer a toast with his *brethren and fathers,* recapping all of Sacred History and "to the health of Salvation!" And their conversation over a glass of wine almost automatically changed into a stoning amid the shards of broken glass. But this complete failure of dialogue is also the victory of witness given to something vaster than all our hopes.

Power of prayer

The true martyr has no other power but prayer. This is what makes him so formidable. Obviously, I am not against taking up physical weapons. It is good to turn the other cheek. Nevertheless, when the other cheek that they are trying to bruise is not your own, but that of your wife or of your children, charity consists of stepping in between and donating a good right hook to the attacker. This is called legitimate defense. It does not break the commandment "You shall not kill," but rather makes people respect it, and therefore, if circumstances demand it, it renders someone who would try to break the commandment incapable of harming others. The Cristeros fought for peace more than the pacifists, who by their passivity made themselves accomplices of the destroyers. Yet they were laymen, peasants, and fathers of families, not priests or monks, because monks and priests—being much more free because of it—battle only with the sword of the word, which is still more powerful than all earthly swords.

He who lives by the sword will perish by the sword (Mt 26:52); he may win fairly, but he nevertheless remains on the adversary's terrain. He is not stronger than violence. The Cristeros knew this: they equipped themselves with pitchforks and shotguns, not to celebrate the power of the pitchfork and the shotgun, but to struggle against a government that tried to forbid them to teach their children the even greater power of prayer. What power is this? Precisely the power of not being on the same level of the power that crushes, of the overwhelming superiority or the brutish domination.

He who must trample and climb over the bodies of little ones in order to establish his rule demonstrates his weakness. The true superior does not strut and preen: he stoops and extends a hand. The Almighty raises up the lowly, and this is why he *puts down the mighty from their thrones* (cf. Lk 1:52). He does not dispute their crown on the same level; he shows them that true power is fruitfulness, not supremacy; that it belongs not to the despot who subdues the populace, but to the father who provides room for his children's future. Whereas the sword commands, prayer demands, and, in asking, nips brutality in the bud, awakens responsibility, and makes the other capable of the decisive choice—either to feel disarmed and to start listening, or to become more enraged and put you on the cross, or else—and this is more common—to start listening after having put you on the cross, because he is astonished by your stubborn insistence on remaining generous in the midst of torment.

Of course, when the cannibal starts cooking you on a spit, you will not necessarily help him improve his barbecue sauce nor persuade him that your flesh is better than veal, but, with the grace of God, you will still make sure that he shares the food equitably with his fellows and tries to say grace before the meal. And when a very pretty seductress starts to caress your thigh—and this is a much more formidable torment—you will not start a discussion about the theology of indissoluble marriage—or you will be lost!—but rather you will turn her down firmly, ask her news about her dad, point out to her that, according to Saint Paul, the loveliest body for you is your wife's, and ask her to get in contact with your young cousin Bertrand who regrets he is still single. Be assured that both the cannibal and the man-eating girl will end up being touched by how strong and extremely well-mannered you are.

More radical than a jihadist

Basically, what you can blame the jihadists most for is their lack of radical commitment. They are ashamed of this, probably, since they feign it by usurping the name of "martyrs"—when they are merely suicides and assassins. I do not blame them so much for proving with a Kalashnikov their total lack of arguments (after all, they do not claim to be college graduates or diplomats). I blame them for not being sufficiently *submissive* to divine Providence.

As a matter of fact, a disciple of the Risen Lord is much more radical than they are. On the one hand, he knows that in order to be a witness to the Resurrection, it is appropriate that he himself should pass by way of Christ's death—which makes him rather indulgent toward his persecutors. On the other hand, he has the assurance that the infidel himself is sent by Allah (since he exists), that he is there to test his faith, and that even despite himself he is a marvelous sign that Allah is great, greater than our ambitions to throttle someone, since his unbelief presupposes a God capable of making, not automatons, but creatures that are free to love him. Finally, if the witness to the Resurrection had to launch an attack in order to shake public opinion, it would be, as much as possible, not by exterminating the living but by reviving consciences that had been long dead, and this takes weapons much more difficult to wield than a sword or a rocket launcher.

Jesus says it solemnly: *When I am lifted up from the earth, I will draw all men to myself* (Jn 12:32). *All men*, including the one who rejects him, because the Risen Lord is nonetheless the basis for his continued existence and the heart of his heart, and anyway a doctor does not make house calls to those who are well. The realism of the faith deprives us of any belief in our privilege. It commands us to profess, while the jihadist knocks us off: I know, despite all appearances, that you are profoundly drawn by Jesus, the eternal Jew, and it may even be that, like Saul after he had eliminated Stephen, you will become for him a *chosen instrument*, better than myself.

EPILOGUE

Not until a manuscript is finished do you realize what book you ought to have written. And when this manuscript furthermore deals with the mystery of God himself, on top of that you recognize that you would have done better to remain silent—or at least to spend all that time in the silence of prayer. May he forgive me my thoughtlessness (and that of my publisher, because, to repeat a remark that could only have pleased Pilate, the one who had the audacity to put this book into your hands, dear reader, is certainly more guilty than I)!

The subject of the Resurrection seemed to me too serious to be treated seriously. Was it appropriate, however, to address it so lightheartedly? Maybe not. I did what I could, especially since, during the composition of many passages, two-year-old Joseph thought he could help my inspiration by climbing on my back, Jacob begged me to watch—right while I was typing *The Resurrection*—an episode of *Curious George*, while my four daughters, when they were not arguing and shouting, were howling gleefully, serenading me at the top of their voices with the song that now arouses murderous instincts in me: "Let It Go" from *Frozen* (not to mention the bills to be paid that surround me, or my wife whose conversation fluctuates incessantly between the sublime and the trivial, one moment asking me: "Do you love me?" and the next: "When are you going to put up the shelves in the laundry?"—but I should think, in spite of appearances, that this is one and the same question).

So that we might be human

Although I have sometimes been whimsical, I don't think that I have been frivolous. One thesis governs this little book—and helps to explain what makes up the possible novelty of its approach. Times have changed. At a moment when, through our connected screens, it seems that anything at all can appear while all doors are closed, it is a matter of understanding that the Risen Lord appears suddenly while all doors are closed to show us that there are still doors to open by knocking on them and turning the doorknob. Apostles nowadays must not just work miracles; they must also restate the obvious, which makes them more ridiculous than ever. They proclaim that fire burns, that night is not day, that the grass does not grow better when you pull on it, that the cow is a herbivore, that a child is born of a man and a woman—in short, that there is an order in reality.

Why the ridicule? Because what yesterday was human destiny—being born a girl or a boy of a father and a mother, working with your hands, sharing a meal around a table, taking your turn at begetting, and then making way for the next generation by leaving this world—all this seems to have been made optional by technology. They already ask us whether we prefer to have a baby through sex or in a test tube (while making us feel that the test tube is more selective and high-performance). Tomorrow they will ask us whether we still want to die or whether we prefer to be immortal (so as to be euthanized delightfully after a few months). Finally, they confront us with this new choice: remain human or be upgraded to an alleged Humanity 2.0.

But while science sends probes into space, *wisdom has set her table* (Prv 9:2). And while the engineer designs a superman, God creates man and woman. This is why the Church today is waging countless battles on unexpected fronts: inspired by the Spirit, she glorifies the flesh; as the depositary of the supernatural, she becomes the guardian of nature; calling people to be holy, she defends sex. And this is why it is no longer enough to say, as in the past: "God became man so that man might become God." It must also be added that God was made man so that man might remain human, and so that in being divinized he might still be even more human.

Faced with counter-annunciations

I have often insisted on what the Book of Revelation presents to us as a counter-annunciation: *The Dragon stood before the Woman who was about to bear a child, that he might devour her child when she brought it forth* (Rv 12:4). How much progress has been made since the day when this verse was written! Now the Dragon doesn't have to wait for the child to be born to start devouring, and better yet: he can manufacture the baby himself in a laboratory, to suit his plans.

Nowadays, to tell the truth, there is not just one counter-annunciation; there are two or three that contradict and reinforce each other. The proclamation of technology: "Nano-, biological, information and communications technologies will come upon you and the power of Engineering will overshadow you with its transparency." The proclamation of Islamism: "The angel of the Lord declared unto Mohammed, and he conceived nothing, but submitted to the dictates of the Qur'an." In view of the first, we can no longer be content to be apologists of spirituality (and drift toward a type of Buddhism); we must also affirm the goodness of the body as it is engendered naturally, even with its capacity to suffer (*See my hands and my feet, that it is I myself; handle me, and see; for a spirit has not flesh and bones as you see that I have,* Lk 24:39). Given the second, we can no longer be content to invoke God, we must also affirm the legitimacy of man in his culture, his freedom, even his aberrations—in other words, with all the weight of history (*And beginning with Moses and all the prophets, he interpreted to them in all the Scriptures the things concerning himself,* Lk 24:27).

What makes it possible to reaffirm these tenets that are so necessary in our age is the mystery of the Incarnation—the mystery in which Spirit takes on flesh, down to its mortal wounds, in which divinity does not abolish but fulfills humanity. And hence the Resurrection appears to us as the thing that surpasses and drives back both Submission and Cybernetization.

In this respect, and increasingly, it is not just the grounds for faith in eternal life; it is also the reason to keep giving temporal life to little mortals. I noted this in the introduction: it is just as impossible to revive oneself as to give birth to oneself—both cases involve a power that transcends me—and the ability to accept absolutely the fact of being born, despite injustice, suffering, and death, despite the historical contingency of not being the pure Me or the one who is spotlessly Submissive, but rather the pathetic son of Danielle and Bernard, contains at least implicitly the faith in a glory that justifies the generations. Today the Resurrection guarantees not only paradise; it also guarantees birth.

The apparitions of the Risen One as our temptation in the desert

The apparitions of the Risen One are spread out over *forty days* (Acts 1:3). After that he effaces himself in the Ascension, and the angels ask the disciples: *Men of Galilee, why do you stand looking into heaven?* (Acts 1:11). They echo what Moses said in the Book of Deuteronomy: *The Torah. . .is not in heaven, that you should say, "Who will go up for us to heaven, and bring it to us, that we may hear it and do it?"* (Dt 30:12). And the angels refer them to the Pentecost that will teach them that Jesus is not elsewhere but right here, in *the Holy Spirit*, the object of *the promise*, who has finally been *poured out* (Acts 2:33).

Some people envy the good fortune of the disciples: They actually saw him, and we do not see him! But to have seen him was also a trial. It was the temptation to cling to him and to freeze in hypnotic fascination—forgetting one's neighbor, not even seeing any more the adventure and the universe he is creating especially for us, along with the miracle of what happens "down the block, on a beach, under a tree," as the song says, and the sun that passes like a hat from head to head. . . . We noticed this temptation especially in Mary Magdalene or in Thomas the Twin. The last lesson of the incarnate Word was to repeat simple gestures and thereby to teach them no longer to see him, but to see all things in him, and to recognize his glory which surfaces everywhere in everyday life.

After the Ascension, heaven and earth exchange their rings, flesh becomes henceforth part of invisible reality, and the Spirit—part of visible reality. The disciples can thus achieve the simplicity that Martin Buber encountered in three rabbis from a Yiddishland that has now vanished: "They spoke about lofty things, very lofty things, but also about the day's events. About the lofty things they spoke as though they were events that might take place in their neighborhood, and about this-worldly events they spoke as though they were woven of some celestial material. In between, they fell silent, but these silences were made up of their common presence."

Praroman, Switzerland, April 12, 2015,
Divine Mercy Sunday